Tough Guy Wisdom III

Revenge of the Tough Guy

Alain Burrese

TGW BOOKS
Missoula, Montana

Also by Alain Burrese:

Books:

Tough Guy Wisdom
Tough Guy Wisdom II: Return of the Tough Guy
Hard-Won Wisdom From The School Of Hard Knocks
Lost Conscience

DVDs:

Hapkido Hoshinsul
Streetfighting Essentials
Hapkido Cane
Lock On: Joint Locking Essentials vols. 1-5

Print ISBN: 978-1-937872-04-5
eBook ISBN: 978-1-937872-05-2

Published by TGW Books, a division of
Burrese Enterprises, Inc.
Missoula, MT 59801, USA

Cover design by Bryan Whitney.

Visit the Tough Guy Wisdom website: www.toughguywisdom.com

DEDICATION

The *Tough Guy Wisdom* series is dedicated to my wife, Yi-saeng, and our daughter, Cosette. If nothing else, I want to be their "Tough Guy."

INTRODUCTION

I grew up watching tough guy movies, and I have to admit, they are still my favorite genre. Of course I watch other movies, but my favorites are watching a tough guy kicking ass and taking names, righting wrongs, punishing those who deserve it, and most of all – saying the lines the mark the epitome of cool, those lines we remember, repeat, and identify with "Tough Guys."

I'd even repeat the lines for real once in a while when younger and frequenting various watering holes and doing my best to be a tough guy. After all, as an Army paratrooper and sniper, I had to live up to those tough guy role models from the silver screen. I even made up my own tough guy line that I used in a bar or two, "You ain't big enough, and you don't have enough friends." Yeah, I thought I was cool, just like my movie heroes.

I'll also admit, it was Rambo in *First Blood* that influenced me to join the Army, go the Airborne and sniper route, and almost re-up to put in a Special Forces packet. I got out instead, and was influenced by Martin Riggs in the first two *Lethal Weapon* movies to head to Los Angeles and apply for the LAPD. (Yes, one could say I let movies influence me too much.) After being in LA for a bit, making the hiring list, and then speaking with an Army buddy's dad who was a Los Angeles fireman, I decided that going to college was a better choice and decided against wearing the Blue in LA.

The *Billy Jack* movies influenced my interest in the martial art of Hapkido. Many people remember this line from *Billy Jack*, "I'm going to take this right foot, and I'm going to wop you on that side of your face. And you want to know something, there's not a damn thing you're going to be able to do about it." At the time, I never knew I'd eventually live and train in South Korea, teach, write about, and do

DVDs on Hapkido, and have the opportunity to train with Grand Master Bong Soo Han, the Korean Hapkido master who performed the actual kick after that famous line. That was definitely a tough guy movie that influenced me in a very positive way.

Now, a bit older and a bit wiser, I don't go out looking for opportunities to use tough guy lines and get in trouble as I used to, but I still enjoy watching tough guy movies, both new ones that come out, and revisiting those of yesteryear that I grew up with. That's why working on the *Tough Guy Wisdom* series has been a lot of fun. I watched every movie to collect the quotes and information for this series. I also used on-line and print sources to find the movie and actor trivia that the books contain. The Internet Movie Database, IMDb, provided much assistance in writing these books. I'm grateful to them all.

Some quotes, such as "What was that?" (found in this volume) don't seem "tough guy," until you have the setting. That's why I included the setting for each quote included in the *Tough Guy Wisdom* series. You need to picture a bad guy saying, "Necht schiessen!" which means "Don't Shoot," to Bruce Willis as John McClane in *Die Hard With a Vengeance* (1995), and then picture McClane shooting the bad guy, and saying to the dead body, "What was that?" It's the wise-cracking and coolness in the face of danger or difficult situations that helps endear us to these tough guy heroes.

You will also notice an absence of a few of the most famous of tough guys, specifically John Wayne, Clint Eastwood, Charles Bronson, Arnold Schwarzenegger, Sylvester Stallone, and Chuck Norris. These six Hollywood tough guys will each have their own specific volume in the *Tough Guy Wisdom* series. So, if you are a fan of any, or all, of these actors - stay tuned. Collections of their most famous quotes, movie trivia, and facts about them will be appearing in special volumes to be released later.

I wrote this third volume along with volumes one and two, so if you see a couple of quotes from one of your favorite tough guy movies, but wonder why a specific quote is missing, it may be in one of the others in the series. Or maybe I missed one that you think should be included. If you have a favorite tough guy movie or quote that you believe should be featured, e-mail me at aburrese@aol.com and it will be considered for a future volume.

I sincerely hope that you enjoy reading these tough guy quotes, along with the movie and actor trivia, as much as I enjoyed collecting them. It's pretty cool when you can tell your wife and friends that watching a tough guy movie is actually work. I'm also sure that reading this book will remind you of movies you saw a long time ago and will want to watch again. Take it from me, it is fun to watch them again and remember the first time you saw them, and reminisce a bit. So relax and enjoy a little bit of *Tough Guy Wisdom*.

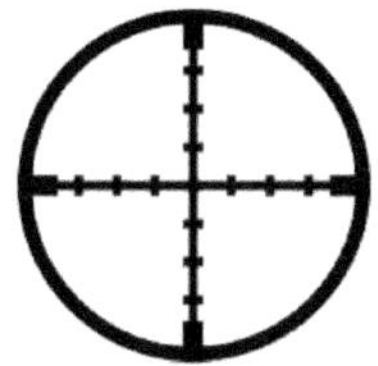

TOUGH GUY WISDOM III
REVENGE OF THE TOUGH GUY

"After I shoot you through the door, you can examine the bullet. Open up."

Mel Gibson as Martin Riggs – ***Lethal Weapon 2 (1989)***

Setting:

Riggs' reply to Leo Getz (Joe Pesci) when he and Murtaugh (Danny Glover) first meet Getz, and Getz asks through the locked door, "How do I know it's the police?"

Movie Trivia:

Joe Pesci, who plays Leo Getz, won an Oscar for Best Actor in a Supporting Role for his part as Tommy DeVito in *Goodfellas* (1990).

About the Actor:

Mel Gibson attended drama school with Judy Davis, who was nominated for Oscars for her roles in *Husbands and Wives* (1992) and *A Passage to India* (1984).

"I got enough friends."

Bruce Willis as Lt. John McClane – ***Die Hard 2 Die Harder (1990)***

Setting:

While fighting on the wing of a moving airplane, controlled by terrorists, Major Grant (John Amos) tells McClane, "Too bad, McClane, I kind of liked you." McClane says the above just before kicking Grant off the wing where Grant gets sucked into one of the jet engines.

Movie Trivia:

John Amos, who plays Major Grant, has a long list of acting credits under his belt, including the popular television series from the 1970s, *Good Times* (1974 -1979), where he played James Evans, Sr. Amos was on the show from 1974 through 1976. His character was one of the first sit-com characters to ever be killed off.

About the Actor:

Bruce Willis once said everyone is becoming too reliant on social networking as a form of talking to each other.

"Take it easy. I'm the good guy."

Steven Seagal as Shane Daniels – ***A Dangerous Man (2009)***

Setting:

After witnessing Chinese mafia henchmen kill a state trooper, Daniels gets involved and kills one of them. Sergey (Jesse Hutch), who also witnessed the ordeal and was shot at by the thug Daniels killed, comes up on the dead body and Daniels with a scared look. This was Daniels' way of trying to reassure him.

Movie Trivia:

In 2009, Keoni Waxman directed two Steven Seagal movies, *The Keeper* (2009) and *A Dangerous Man* (2009).

About the Actor:

Steven Seagal and Arissa Wolf have one daughter, Savannah.

"There was only three of them."

Sam Elliott as Wade Garrett – ***Road House (1989)***

Setting:

Garrett's reply when he comes staggering, and beat up, into the Double Deuce and Dalton (Patrick Swayze) asks him, "Are you all right?"

Movie Trivia:

In the same year Sam Elliott played a tough guy bouncer in *Road House* (1989), he appeared in the family Christmas movie *Prancer* (1989).

About the Actor:

Samuel Pack Elliott was born in Sacramento, California, on August 9, 1944.

"The future is right now."

Kurt Russell as Snake Plissken – ***Escape From L.A. (1996)***

Setting:

When Taslima (Valeria Golino) comes on to Snake and invites him to her place, she tells him, "I'll read your future." With the above comment, he walks off toward his mission.

Movie Trivia:

Escape From L.A. (1996) is one of five movies Steve Buscemi appeared in during 1996. He played Map to the Stars Eddie in *Escape From L.A.* (1996), Johnny Flynn in *Kansas City* (1996), Tommy in *Trees Lounge* (1996), The Father in *Black Kites* (1996), and Carl Showalter in the award winning Coen Brothers' hit *Fargo* (1996).

About the Actor:

Kurt Russell helped John Carpenter and Debra Hill write *Escape From L.A.* (1996).

"There's always barber college."

Patrick Swayze as Dalton – ***Road House (1989)***

Setting:

After telling Morgan (Terry Funk) he's out of there because he doesn't have the right temperament for the trade, Morgan asks Dalton what he's supposed to do. This was Dalton's reply and the beginning of his speech to the employees of the Double Deuce.

Movie Trivia:

Terry Funk, who plays Morgan in *Road House* (1989), has appeared in a number of movies, but he is probably most known for his career as a professional wrestler.

About the Actor:

Patrick Swayze studied with Warren Robertson, one of the best acting coaches in New York, when he decided he wanted to continue performing, even though his ballet career was over.

"You know what I think I'm gonna do then? Just for the hell of it. ("Tell me." – Posner) I'm gonna take this right foot, and I'm gonna whop you on that side of your face. And you wanna know something? There's not a damn thing you're gonna be able to do about it."

Tom Laughlin as Billy Jack – ***Billy Jack (1971)***

Setting:

In the park, Posner (Bert Freed) tells Billy he doesn't have a choice, and after Billy tells Posner what he's going to do, Posner asks, "Really?" Billy replies, "Really," and kicks him with a reverse crescent kick in the face like he said he would.

Movie Trivia:

Hapkido master Bong Soo Han performed the actual kick that whopped Posner in the face, as he doubled for Tom Laughlin for some of the fight scenes. Grandmaster Han also choreographed the fight scenes.

About the Actor:

Tom Laughlin trained with fight choreographer and hapkido master Bong Soo Han for his fight scenes in *Billy Jack* (1971), but the hapkido master doubled for him for the more difficult kicks.

"Yeah I am, it covers my body."

Robert De Niro as Sam – ***Ronin (1998)***

Setting:

When Sam asks questions about how many they will be facing and how they will be getting back after the operation, Spence (Sean Bean) asks him, "You worried about saving your own skin?" This is Sam's reply.

Movie Trivia:

Three of the actors from *Ronin* (1998) played villains in 007 James Bond films: Sean Bean in *GoldenEye* (1995), Michael Lonsdale in *Moonraker* (1979), and Jonathan Pryce in *Tomorrow never Dies* (1997).

About the Actor:

Robert De Niro's birth name was Robert Mario De Niro Jr.

"In my line of work Eddie, we have excuses for all kinds of bad behavior. But a man's a man. How he carries himself is all I'm concerned about. I don't judge people Eddie. I just don't like you."

Eric Roberts as Merle "The Butcher" Henche – ***The Butcher (2007)***

Setting:

Henche's response when Eddie Hellstrom (Jerry Trimble Jr.) asks why he doesn't like him.

Movie Trivia:

Jerry Trimble Jr., who plays Eddie in *The Butcher* (2007), portrays Mickey in *Charlie Valentine* (2009) and the last human cop in *The Last Sentinel* (2007). All three movies were directed by Jesse V. Johnson.

About the Actor:

Eric Roberts appeared with Cheech Marin (minus Tommy Chong) in *Rude Awakening* (1989).

"Don't wait for it to happen, don't even want it to happen. Just watch what does happen."

Sean Connery as Jim Malone – ***The Untouchables (1987)***

Setting:

Malone acts as a tutor and provides some advice to Ness (Kevin Costner) and the others while waiting in a small cabin on a stake out near the Canadian border.

Movie Trivia:

The Untouchables (1987) received one Oscar and three other Oscar nominations. Won: Best Actor in a Supporting Role, Sean Connery. Nominated: Best Art Direction-Set Decoration, Patrizia von Brandenstein, William A. Elliott, and Hal Gausman; Best Costume Design, Marilyn Vance; Best Music, Original Score, Ennio Morricone.

About the Actor:

Sean Connery won a Life Achievement Award from the American Film Institute in 2006.

"Ed, what an ugly thing to say. I abhor ugliness. Does this mean we're not friends anymore? You know, Ed, if I thought you weren't my friend, I just don't think I could bear it."

Val Kilmer as Doc Holliday – ***Tombstone (1993)***

Setting:

Holliday's reply to Ed Bailey (Frank Stallone) during a poker game he just won when Bailey says, "Them guns don't scare me, because without them guns you ain't nothing but a skinny lunger." Holliday then places his guns on the table and says, "There. Now we can be friends again." Bailey attacks him and Holliday uses his knife.

Movie Trivia:

Frank Stallone, who plays Ed Bailey, is Sylvester Stallone's brother. His first four film appearances were as singers in his brother's movies: *Rocky* (1976), *Paradise Alley* (1978), *Rocky II* (1979), and *Rocky III* (1982).

About the Actor:

Val Kilmer was born on December 31, 1959.

"My first thought would be … a lot."

Nicolas Cage as Cameron Poe – ***Con Air (1997)***

Setting:

Poe's reply to Mike 'Baby-O' O'Dell (Mykelti Williamson) who asked, "What's wrong with him?" O'Dell was asking about Garland 'The Marietta Mangler' Greene (Steve Buscemi), who has just commented about William 'Billy Bedlam' Bedford (Nick Chinlund) by saying, "He's a fountain of misplaced rage. Name your cliché. Mother held him too much, or not enough. Last picked at kick ball, late-night sneaky uncle. Whatever. Now he's so angry, moments of levity actually cause him pain. Give him headaches. Happiness for that gentleman hurts."

Movie Trivia:

Garland 'The Marietta Mangler' Greene (Steve Buscemi) survives the plane crash and avoids authorities, and is last seen playing craps where when asked if the new shooter feels lucky, replies, "Yes… yes he does."

About the Actor:

Nicolas Cage was married to Lisa Marie Presley (Elvis Presley's daughter) for only a few months before the couple filed for divorce.

"We need emotional content... I said emotional content, not anger... Don't think! Feel! It is like a finger pointing a way to the moon. Don't concentrate on the finger or you will miss all that heavenly glory."

Bruce Lee as Lee – ***Enter the Dragon (1973)***

Setting:

Lee stops his conversation with Mr. Braithwaite (Geoffrey Weeks) to provide a lesson to one of the students, by telling Braithwaite, "It's Lao's (Wei Tung) time." This was the lesson Lee taught.

Movie Trivia:

Enter the Dragon (1973) was directed by Robert Clouse, who also directed *Game of Death* (1978), *The Big Brawl* (1980), *Force Five* (1981), *Gymkata* (1985), and *China O'Brien* (1990), among other films and television shows.

About the Actor:

Bruce Lee had a number of notable students, including James Coburn, Steve McQueen, and Lee Marvin. McQueen and Coburn were also pallbearers at Lee's funeral.

"One twitch, and you're in hell!"

Robert Duvall as Boss Spearman – ***Open Range (2003)***

Setting:

Boss Spearman's first command to the bad guys when he and Charley Waite (Kevin Costner) confront the hooded riders at their camp, attempting to prevent the bad guys from stampeding their herd. Unfortunately, while Spearman and Waite confront this group, others are attacking Mose (Abraham Benrubi) and Button (Diego Luna) back at their camp.

Movie Trivia:

Beyond the Open Range (2004) is the documentary describing the filming of the movie.

About the Actor:

After a two year hitch in the army, Robert Duvall attended The Neighborhood Playhouse School of the Theatre in New York City on the G.I. Bill. While there, Duvall shared an apartment with Dustin Hoffman and was friends with another struggling young actor named Gene Hackman.

"Well, you've got me quaking in my boots, but I'm still gonna bring you down."

Mel Gibson as Martin Riggs – ***Lethal Weapon 2 (1989)***

Setting:

Riggs' reply to Arjen Rudd (Joss Ackland) after Rudd informs him that he will be taking up the serious diplomatic situation with the State Department the next day, after the arrest is halted because Rudd's diplomatic agent identity had been established.

Movie Trivia:

Martin Riggs refers to the famous line from the *Lethal Weapon* films when he tells Murtaugh, "Oh, I'm sorry, I forgot. You're too old for this shit," after fellow police officers gave Murtaugh the Rubber Plant as a joke about Murtaugh's daughter being in a condom commercial.

About the Actor:

Mel Gibson played Hamlet in Shakespeare's classic tale of vengeance and tragedy, *Hamlet* (1990).

"This career chooses the man. Ain't the other way around."

Tom Berenger as Thomas Beckett – ***Sniper (1993)***

Setting:

Beckett's reply to Richard Miller (Billy Zane) when he states, "It may be your career choice but it ain't mine."

Movie Trivia:

The weapon used by Becket is an M40A1 Sniper Rifle which is based on the Remington Model 700 Bolt Action Rifle.

About the Actor:

Tom Berenger studied acting in New York at the Herbert Berghof Studios.

"I'm not having any fun here. You know how cranky I get when I don't have any fun."

Tommy Lee Jones as Chief Deputy Marshal Samuel Gerard – ***U.S. Marshals (1998)***

Setting:

Gerard tells his team they need to get moving on the John Doe who escaped from the crashed plane. The John Doe is Mark J. Sheridan (Wesley Snipes).

Movie Trivia:

John Pogue, who wrote *U.S. Marshals* (1998), was also the writer for *The Skulls* (2000), *The Skulls II* (2002), and *The Skulls III* (2003).

About the Actor:

Tommy Lee Jones made his film debut in 1970. The movie was *Love Story* (1970) starring Ali MacGraw and Ryan O'Neal. Tommy Lee Jones played Hank Simpson.

"Yippee-ki-yay, motherfucker."

Bruce Willis as John McClane – ***Die Hard With a Vengeance (1995)***

Setting:

McClane just watched the helicopter with Simon Gruber (Jeremy Irons) and other bad guys crash and explode as he reprises his famous line from the first two movies.

Movie Trivia:

There are two solutions to the water jug riddle in the park, at the elephant fountain, to disarm the bomb. Here is one of them. To place exactly 4 gallons of water on the scales when you only have two jugs which hold 3 and 5 gallons respectively, you: **1.** Fill the 5 gallon jug and decant the water into the 3 gallon jug. This leaves 2 gallons in the big jug. **2.** Empty the 3 gallon jug and pour in the 2 gallons from the 5 gallon jug, leaving space for 1 gallon in the small jug. **3.** Refill the 5 gallon jug and pour water from it into the 3 gallon jug until the small jug is full. **4.** That leaves exactly four gallons in the big jug; put it on the scale and the bomb is disarmed.

About the Actor:

The Bruce Willis *Die Hard* catch phrase "Yippee-Ki-Yay" inspired Eric Lichtenfeld to write an article titled, "Yippee-Ki-Yay… The greatest one-liner in movie history."

"Brother, life's a bitch, and she's back in heat."

"Rowdy" Roddy Piper as Nada – ***They Live (1988)***

Setting:

After beating each other senseless, Nada finally gets Frank (Keith David) to try on the glasses that reveal the aliens and subliminal messages. This is Nada's line to Frank as he looks around in bewilderment.

Movie Trivia:

Piper's character is listed as Nada in the credits, but his name is never spoken in the movie.

About the Actor:

In 2003, Roddy Piper came out with his autobiography published by Penguin-Putnam, titled, *In the Pit with Piper.*

"Then you're kind of dumb to be drinking here, ain't ya?"

Gregory Peck as Jimmy Ringo – ***The Gunfighter (1950)***

Setting:

Ringo's reply to Hunt Bromley (Skip Homeier) when he says, "I say Mac (Karl Malden) waters his whiskey." As the conversation progresses, Bromley is surprised that Ringo has heard about him. Ringo states, "Yeah, I heard about ya. I heard you're a cheap, no-good, barroom loafer. If I didn't have something else on my mind, I'd take them guns away from ya and slap ya cross-eyed." Bromley replies, "You're asking for trouble Mr. Ringo." The conversation continues with Ringo telling Bromley, "Well, you already got it pardner. Cause I got a gun on you under the table. And it's pointing smack at your belly. Now you gonna get out of here or not?" Bromley says he's disappointed. Ringo tells him, "The older you grow, the more you learn, son. Now turn around and head for the door."

Movie Trivia:

The Gunfighter (1950) was directed by Henry King, who also directed *Twelve O'clock High* (1949), *The Snows of Kilimanjaro* (1952), and *Tender Is the Knight* (1962) among others.

About the Actor:

In 1943, Gregory Peck debuted in the RKO film *Days of Glory* (1944) as Vladimir.

"I believe you. But it's not gonna save you."

Liam Neeson as Bryan Mills – ***Taken (2008, US release 2009)***

Setting:

Said to Marko (Arben Barjraktaraj), the kidnapper he has been torturing for information about who they sold his daughter to, just before turning on the electricity one last time and walking away.

Movie Trivia:

Taken (2008, US release 2009) was nominated for a 2010 Saturn Award for Best International Film from the Academy of Science Fiction, Fantasy & Horror Films.

About the Actor:

Liam Neeson was married to Natasha Richardson from July 3, 1994 to March 18, 2009, when she tragically died from a head injury she received from a fall while skiing.

"You know, the right way to do things isn't always the lawful way."

*Treat Williams as Karl Thomasson – **The Substitute 3: Winner Takes All (1999)***

Setting:

Thomasson discusses the situation regarding the football players and drug dealing with Prof. Nicole Stewart (Rebecca Staab).

Movie Trivia:

Rebecca Staab, who played Prof. Nicole Stewart, has a long list of television credits, including shows such as *Nip/Tuck* (2004), *CSI: NY* (2005), *Las Vegas* (2007), *The Cleaner* (2008), *The Young and the Restless* (2008) and *Desperate Housewives* (2009).

About the Actor:

Treat Williams has been married to Pam Van Sant since 1988.

"Water's wet. The sky is blue. Women have secrets. Who gives a fuck?"

Bruce Willis as Joe Hallenbeck – ***The Last Boy Scout (1991)***

Setting:

In their first meeting, Hallenbeck is confronted by Jimmy Dix (Damon Wayans) in the strip club because he has been paid to keep an eye on Dix's girlfriend Cory (Halle Berry), and Dix didn't know about it. This is what Hallenbeck tells him about the "secret."

Movie Trivia:

Halle Berry's part was small in this 1991 action movie, but the same year she also had roles in *Jungle Fever* (1991) and *Strictly Business* (1991). Prior to these three movies, she had only appeared in a few television shows.

About the Actor:

Bruce Willis worked a short time as a private investigator. He played a private investigator in both the television series *Moonlighting* (1985 – 1989) and the movie *The Last Boy Scout* (1991).

"Aim small, miss small."

Mel Gibson as Benjamin Martin – ***The Patriot (2000)***

Setting:

Martin's instructions about shooting to his sons as they prepare to rescue their older brother who was taken by the British.

Movie Trivia:

It's reported that the line "Aim small, miss small" came from advice technical advisor Mark Baker gave to Mel Gibson and Heath Ledger when teaching them to shoot muzzle-loading rifles. Gibson liked the advice and incorporated it into the movie.

About the Actor:

Mel Gibson was chosen by *People* magazine as one of the "50 Most Beautiful People" in the world in 1990, 1991, and 1996.

"You kind of talk to much, you know."

Steven Seagal as Lt. Jack Cole – ***The Glimmer Man (1996)***

Setting:

Cole enters a restaurant to visit with Mr. Smith (Brian Cox), while the host is telling someone on the phone they are closed. When the host calls Cole a name, Cole slaps him to the ground and tells the person on the phone to come on down for a table.

Movie Trivia:

Brian Cox, who plays Mr. Smith, was the first actor to play Dr. Hannibal Lecter in the film *Manhunter* (1986).

About the Actor:

Steven Seagal attended Buena Park High School in Buena Park, California.

"Okay, you people sit tight, hold the fort, and keep the home fires burning, and if we're not back by dawn, call the president."

*Kurt Russell as Jack Burton – **Big Trouble in Little China (1986).***

Setting:

After declaring, "I'm a reasonable guy, but I've just experienced unreasonable things," and telling them he can take the truth, Burton tells Gracie Law (Kim Cattrall) and others that he will go with Wang Chi (Dennis Dun) to help save Miao Yin (Suzee Pai).

Movie Trivia:

Kim Cattrall, who played Gracie Law, is widely known for her role as Samantha Jones in *Sex and the City* (1998 – 2004) and the movies that followed the television series.

About the Actor:

After kicking Elvis in the shin in *It Happened at the World's Fair* (1963), Kurt Russell played Elvis Presley in his first collaboration with John Carpenter in *Elvis* (1979).

"I figured you'd rather be shot by me than by him."

Kevin Spacey as Lt. Chris Sabian – ***The Negotiator (1998)***

Setting:

As they are about to take Roman (Samuel L. Jackson) away in an ambulance at the end of the movie, Sabian apologizes for shooting him, but figures a wounding shot was better than letting Frost (Ron Rifkin) shoot and kill Roman.

Movie Trivia:

The movie was written to star Sylvester Stallone and Kevin Spacey, with Spacey as the hostage taker and Stallone playing the opposite role. When Stallone turned the project down, Spacey decided he wanted the other part and his original role went to Samuel L. Jackson.

About the Actor:

Kevin Spacey Fowler was born on July 26, 1959, in South Orange, New Jersey, USA.

"I said you're under arrest. You have the right to remain silent. You have the right to an attorney. You have the right to be dead."

Brandon Lee as Johnny Murata – ***Showdown In Little Tokyo (1991)***

Setting:

Officer Murata recites his version of Miranda as he fights with a bad guy; finally kicking him into a large vat of flammable liquid and exploding it with his lighter.

Movie Trivia:

Showdown In Little Tokyo (1991) was Brandon Lee's first starring role in an American film not for television.

About the Actor:

Brandon Bruce Lee was born February 1, 1965, in Oakland, California, USA.

"Look, Lance, there's a time to turn it on."

Brian Bosworth as Joe Huff/John Stone – ***Stone Cold (1991)***

Setting:

Joe Huff tells FBI Agent Lance (Sam McMurray) that he is going to stop the semi with drugs and go back to the gang to stop them from cracking the whip (Killing Senator Brent Whipperton (David Tress)).

Movie Trivia:

Brian Bosworth was nominated for a Razzie Award for Worst New Star for *Stone Cold* (1991).

About the Actor:

Due to a shoulder injury, Brian Bosworth's Seattle Seahawks football years came to an end after three short years. He then took up acting and *Stone Cold* (1991) was his first starring role.

"English 101."

Kurt Russell as Gabe Cash – ***Tango & Cash (1989)***

Setting:

Cash decides to teach the Chinese man, who tried to kill him, English in the restroom. With a chair across his throat, he learns very quick. When another cop comes in and sees Cash sitting on the chair across the bad guy's throat, he asks, "What is this?" The above is Cash's answer.

Movie Trivia:

Tango & Cash (1989) was directed by Andrei Konchalovsky. He also directed *Runaway Train* (1985) with Jon Voight, Eric Roberts, and Rebecca De Mornay. However, he was replaced toward the end of principal photography on *Tango & Cash* (1989) due to creative reasons. He was replaced by Albert Magnoli.

About the Actor:

In 1989, besides *Tango & Cash* (1989), Kurt Russell also appeared as Wayland Jackson in *Winter People* (1989).

"God, I'm enjoying this."

Tom Berenger as Jonathan Shale – ***The Substitute (1996)***

Setting:

Shale chases Matt Wolfson (Cliff De Young) into a locker room to gain information from him. He is smacking Wolfson around with a helmet when he says this, and then tells him to leave the country before he becomes unreasonable.

Movie Trivia:

Raymond Cruz, who plays Joey Six, the only team member to survive and walk off in the credits with Berenger, also played Detective Julio Sanchez in the television series *The Closer* (2005 – 2011).

About the Actor:

In 1993, Tom Berenger was nominated for Outstanding Guest Actor in a Comedy Series for his role as Don Santry in *Cheers* (1993).

"You know mister, if I'd brought a pretty lady like that into a place like this, I'd stay close."

Scott Glenn as Emmett – ***Silverado (1995)***

Emmett's reply to the young man in the wagon train who does not trust Emmett and his companions to find the men who stole the wagon train's gold and bring it back, and stated that he did not plan on letting Emmett and his companions out of his site.

Movie Trivia:

In 1999, the cast and crew members recalled making *Silverado* (1985) in the documentary, "The Making of Silverado."

About the Actor:

Scott Glenn was bedridden for a year as a youth, and doctors predicted he would limp for the rest of his life. He got rid of his limp by challenging his illness with intense training programs.

"It's not in your face. It's in my hand."

Robert Downey Jr. as Sherlock Holmes – ***Sherlock Holmes (2009)***

Setting:

Holmes' reply while talking to Dr. John Watson (Jude Law), when he points a violin bow in Watson's face and Watson says, "Get that out of my face." After the above quote, Watson replies to Holmes, "Get what's in your hand out of my face."

Movie Trivia:

Watson's (Jude Law) line to Holmes (Robert Downey Jr.), "You know that what you're drinking is for eye surgery," is an obscure reference to Holmes' cocaine usage. At the time, cocaine was used as a topical anesthetic for eye surgery. In the stories, Holmes injects cocaine.

About the Actor:

Robert Downey Jr. was nominated for a Saturn Award for Best Actor in *Sherlock Holmes* (2009).

"Ask any racer, any real racer. It don't matter if you win by an inch or a mile. Winning's winning."

*Vin Diesel as Dominic Toretto – **The Fast and the Furious (2001)***

Setting:

Toretto's reply to Brian O'Conner (Paul Walker) after the first race when O'Conner says he almost had him.

Movie Trivia:

The Fast and the Furious (2001) was directed by Rob Cohen, who appeared as the Pizza Hut delivery guy in a cameo right before the first big race.

About the Actor:

Vin Diesel accidentally broke a stuntman's nose filming *The Fast and the Furious* (2001).

"Drop it, dickhead. It's the police."

Bruce Willis as John McClane – ***Die Hard (1988)***

Setting:

John McClane gets the drop on Karl's (Alexander Godunov) brother, the first of the terrorists he confronts and eliminates.

Movie Trivia:

Die Hard (1988) was nominated for four Oscars: Best Film Editing, Frank J. Urioste, John F. Link; Best Sound, Don J. Bassman, Kevin F. Cleary, Richard Overton, Al Overton Jr.; Best Sound Effects Editing, Stephen Hunter Flick, Richard Shorr; Best Visual Effects, Richard Edlund, Al Di Sarro, Brent Boates, Thaine Morris.

About the Actor:

Bruce Willis is among the people in the courtroom during the closing speech of *The Verdict* (1982) starring Paul Newman and nominated for Best Picture.

"You die first, get it? Your friends might get me in a rush but not before I make your head into a canoe. You understand me?"

Kurt Russell as Wyatt Earp – ***Tombstone (1993)***

Setting:

After Curly Bill Brocius (Powers Booth) kills Marshal Fred White (Harry Carey Jr.), Earp knocks Curly Bill out and says he'll go to trial as the Clanton's come to take him away. He holds his gun to Ike Clanton's (Stephen Lang) forehead and says the above to show he means business. When Billy Clanton (Thomas Haden Church) says he's bluffing and they should rush him, Ike replies, "No, he ain't bluffing." Earp's response, "You're not as stupid as you look, Ike. Now tell them to get back."

Movie Trivia:

Due to an injury, Robert Mitchum was unable to play the part of Old Man Clanton. The part was eliminated from the script and Mitchum provides the narration at the beginning and end of the film.

About the Actor:

Kurt Russell was born in Springfield, Massachusetts, U.S.A.

"This is what I call the speech, kid. It's the only one I've got, I only give it once, so pay attention. Until now, it's all been fun and games, cops and robbers, Dunkin' Donuts, but you're in the shit now. Metro Command is a war zone... They say you're good at what you do, but the team comes first. You live by that, and you'll be okay, and we'll all be there for you. Remember, the door swings both ways. That's it. Hey kid, welcome to the war."

Danny Glover as Lt. Mike Harrigan – ***Predator 2 (1990)***

Setting:

Lt. Harrigan gives the welcoming speech to new officer Jerry Lambert (Bill Paxton).

Movie Trivia:

Bill Paxton, who played Jerry Lambert, faced both predators in *Predator 2* (1990) and aliens in *Aliens* (1986), before they faced each other in *AVP: Alien vs Predator* (2004) and *AVPR: Aliens vs Predator – Requiem* (2007). It is said he was approached for *AVPR* so he could be in the second movie of all three series, but scheduling conflicts prevented him from making an appearance.

About the Actor:

Danny Glover was cast as the lead in *Predator 2* (1990) after Arnold Schwarzenegger declined to appear in the sequel.

"Everything they want from here on out, they're gonna have to take. You don't understand that do you?"

Tom Laughlin as Billy Jack – ***Billy Jack (1971)***

Setting:

In the barn with a bullet wound in his side, after killing Deputy Mike (Ken Tobey), Jean (Delores Taylor) tries to talk Billy into giving himself up. This was his reply when she said, "I don't supposed you care too much that you're bleeding to death." She then replies that she doesn't understand, and that you can't solve everything with violence. She then tells Billy she loves him and it's a lot easier to die than to keep on trying.

Movie Trivia:

In the original script, Billy Jack goes down in a blaze of gunfire and glory. Delores Taylor argued against having the lead character killed, and the ending was changed, which allowed for two sequels to be made. However, it was not sequels that prompted Taylor's position as much as her belief that such an ending was not appropriate and would be too painful for the audience.

About the Actor:

Tom Laughlin and Delores Taylor married on October 15, 1954.

"Who's fucking next? McAllister! Who's next?"

Mel Gibson as Sergeant Martin Riggs – ***Lethal Weapon (1987)***

Setting:

Riggs looks for General Peter McAllister (Mitch Ryan), or more of his troops, after escaping from his torturer, Endo (Al Leong). Riggs already killed five of them to rescue Murtaugh (Danny Glover) and Murtaugh's daughter, Rianne (Tracie Wolfe).

Movie Trivia:

The torturer, Endo, was played by Al Leong, an Asian American actor and stuntman who has numerous appearances in action flicks, including *Die Hard* (1988) and *The Scorpion King* (2002).

About the Actor:

Mel Gibson was considered for the role of James Bond in *Golden Eye* (1995).

"We're not running. We're eluding."

Sean Connery as Capt. John Connor – ***Rising Sun (1993)***

Setting:

Conner and Lt. Webster Smith (Wesley Snipes) are being followed, and then pursued, by a blue car. This is Connor's response to Smith's inquiry as to why they are running, after all, they are the cops.

Movie Trivia:

It is reported that writers Michael Crichton and Michael Backes quit the project largely over disagreement with director Philip Kaufman that one of the lead characters should be changed into an African-American.

About the Actor:

The official website for Sir Sean Connery is www.seanconery.com.

"Yeah, well, either you're part of the problem or you're part of the solution, or you're just part of the landscape."

Robert De Niro as Sam – ***Ronin (1998)***

Setting:

Sam's reply to Deirdre (Natascha McElhone) when she says, "I see you're reviewing our problem." The group is in an apartment and Sam is preparing for the operation.

Movie Trivia:

Natascha McElhone, who plays Deirdre, played Karen in the series, *Californication* (2007 – 2012).

About the Actor:

Robert De Niro was married to Diahnne Abbot from 1976 to 1988. De Niro adopted her daughter from a previous marriage, Drena, and the two had a son, Raphael De Niro.

"I want you to be nice, until it's time to not be nice."

Patrick Swayze as Dalton – ***Road House (1989)***

Setting:

Dalton provides a little extra guidance regarding his rule number three: be nice. When an employee asks how they will know when that is, Dalton replies, "You won't. I'll let you know. You are the bouncers. I am the cooler."

Movie Trivia:

In 1990, *Road House* (1989) was nominated for five Razzie Awards: Worse Actor (Patrick Swayze, also for *Next of Kin* (1989)); Worst Director (Rowdy Herrington); Worst Picture (Joel Silver); Worst Screenplay (David Lee Henry and Hilary Henkin); and Worst Supporting Actor (Ben Gazzara).

About the Actor:

Patrick Swayze lost his battle with pancreatic cancer and passed away on September 14, 2009, after a twenty-month fight with the deadly disease.

"Well, unfortunately, in the fabricating of your plans, you inadvertently stepped into my mine field. And to answer the second part of your question, I want you dead."

Steven Seagal as Shane Daniels – ***A Dangerous Man (2009)***

Setting:

Daniel's reply during the final confrontation, when the Colonel (Byron Mann) asks, "Who are you? What do you want?"

Movie Trivia:

Byron Mann, who played the Colonel, also appeared as Wesley in *Catwoman* (2004) with Halle Berry, Quan in *Sniper 3* (2004) with Tom Berenger, and as Sunti in another Steven Seagal picture: *Belly of the Beast* (2003).

About the Actor:

Steven Seagal was married to actress Kelly LeBrock from 1987 to 1996. LeBrock speaks very negatively about the relationship.

"Sure I do. Do you Doyle? Do you have any idea who you're dealing with?"

Eric Roberts as Merle "The Butcher" Henche – ***The Butcher (2007)***

Setting:

Henche walks into Doyle's (Paul Dillon) office and drops his bodyguard with a couple of quick strikes, one of them to the throat. Doyle, sitting behind his desk, asks, "Do you have any idea who you're dealing with here Mr. Henche?" Henche removes one of his guns from the shoulder holster under his jacket and replies with the above.

Movie Trivia:

The tag line for *The Butcher* (2009) is "Never gamble when you are desperate."

About the Actor:

Eric Roberts made his New York stage debut in *Rebel Women* in 1976 when he was 20 years old.

"Don't let the door hit ya where the good Lord split ya."

Steve Austin as John Brickner – ***Damage (2009)***

Setting:

Brickner comments to one of two men he physically throws out of the bar where he works. The two were fighting, and once outside, Brickner tells the two, "See you tomorrow night."

Movie Trivia:

Donnelly Rhodes, who plays Deacon, appeared as Dr. Cottle in 36 episodes of *Battlestar Galactica* (2004 – 2009).

About the Actor:

Steve Austin's birth name was Steve Anderson, the second brother in an eventual line of four brothers and one little sister.

"When you shoot, you always shoot to kill. It's not like the movies. You've got about half a second to figure out what needs to be done."

Tom Selleck as Jesse Stone – ***Stone Cold (2005)***

Setting:

In the bedroom, Abby Taylor (Polly Shannon) asks Stone about a time when he shot someone and killed him. After his reply, she then says, "I guess you need to be that way if you're a policeman." Stone replies, "Maybe I'm a policeman because I am that way."

Movie Trivia:

John Fasano and Michael Brandman are credited with the teleplay for *Stone Cold* (2005), based on Robert B. Parker's novel.

About the Actor:

Director Robert Harmon says Tom Selleck is unbelievably hard working and unbelievably well prepared.

"What's keeping me from reaching over there and kicking the shit out of you?"

John Cena as Det. Danny Fisher – ***12 Rounds (2009)***

Setting:

Fisher questions Miles Jackson (Aidan Gillen) regarding the authenticity of the bomb strapped to Fisher's fiancée, Molly Porter (Ashley Scott), as the three of them ride on a city bus. Jackson replies, "Nothing." But he knows Fisher won't try anything in case the bomb is real.

Movie Trivia:

In the gag reel on the DVD, Director Renny Harlan states, "This is our life when we are making these movies. We work very, very long hours, very hard, but if you make it so serious that everybody's uncomfortable on the set, then it feels like it's just a hardship, then there's no reason to do it."

About the Actor:

Ashley Scott, who played Molly Porter in *12 Rounds* (2009), says John Cena has a great sense of humor.

"My instincts are to wax your ass all over this floor."

Wesley Snipes as John Cutter – ***Passenger 57 (1992)***

Setting:

Cutter has Charles Rane (Bruce Payne) up against the wall as they negotiate whether they will let Rane back on the plane to save the hostages. When Cutter asks if he's supposed to trust Rane, Rane replies, "Trust your instincts." This is Cutter's response.

Movie Trivia:

Bruce Payne, who played Charles 'The Rane of Terror' Rane, also played The Devil in Blake Edwards' *Switch* (1991).

About the Actor:

Wesley Snipes' first big-budget action flick was *Passenger 57* (1992).

"Still playing by the rules, Sheriff?"

Phillip Rhee as Tommy Lee – ***Best of the Best 3: No Turning Back (1995)***

Setting:

When Tommy Lee arrives at his sister Karen's (Cristina Lawson) house to find her beat up, and her son and another boy kidnapped, he asks the above question to his brother-in-law, Sheriff Jack Banning (Christopher McDonald). The two then proceed to break the rules to get the boys back.

Movie Trivia:

Phillip Rhee was one of the producers for *Best of the Best 3: No Turning Back* (1995).

About the Actor:

Phillip Rhee was the only actor from the first two *Best of the Best* movies to appear in *Best of the Best 3: No Turning Back* (1995). However, his brother, Simon Rhee, who played Dae Han in the first two films, was the stunt coordinator on this film as he was on the first two.

"Oh, roadkill."

Patrick Swayze as Jack Crews – ***Black Dog (1998)***

Setting:

Crews comments after a bad guy on a motorcycle, trying to stop the truck he's driving, wipes out.

Movie Trivia:

Black Dog (1998) was directed by Kevin Hooks, who also directed tough guy movie *Passenger 57* (1992) with Wesley Snipes.

About the Actor:

Patrick Swayze's film debut was as Ace Johnson in *Skatetown, U. S. A.* (1979), which starred Scot Baio and also featured Maureen McCormick from *The Brady Bunch* (1969 – 1974).

"For most of my life I made my own rules. You don't do any favors. You don't ask for any. Watch the percentages. But you can know the rules and still do the wrong thing. The only thing I knew for sure was this … Strozzi, Doyle, and every son-of-a-bitch that worked for them, they were all going to be better off dead."

Bruce Willis as John Smith – ***Last Man Standing (1996)***

Setting:

Smith Narrates as he is seen loading his model 1911 .45s.

Movie Trivia:

Film critic Roger Ebert's review of the movie included, "This is such a sad, lonely movie."

About the Actor:

Bruce Willis was born in Idar-Oberstein, West Germany.

"Wrong bet."

Jean-Claude Van Damme as Lyon Gaultier – ***Lionheart (1990)***

Setting:

Lyon's reply to Joshua (Harrison Page) during the final fight against Attila (Abdel Qissi). Joshua tries to get Lyon to throw in the towel and quit, and tells him, "Look. It's on him, man. The whole bet's on Attila."

Movie Trivia:

In Australia, *Lionheart* (1990) was known as "Wrong Bet." The film also featured Billy Blanks (many movies as well as *Tae-Bo* fame) as an African Legionnaire, and Jeff Speakman (*The Perfect Weapon* (1991), etc.) as a Mansion Security Man.

About the Actor:

Jean-Claude Van Damme, along with Frank Dux and Michel Qissi, is listed as a fight choreographer on *Lionheart* (1990).

"No I'm not. I'm just good at it."

Burt Reynolds as Nick 'Mex' Escalante – ***Heat (1986)***

Setting:

Escalante's reply to Cyrus Kinnick (Peter MacNicol) when he states, "You're probably basically a violent man."

Movie Trivia:

The tag line from the movie poster was "Nick Escalante isn't a violent man by nature. He's just good at it."

About the Actor:

Burt Reynolds appeared as the centerfold in *Cosmopolitan* magazine in April, 1972. The centerfold was more recently seen used in ads for DirectTV.

"The fight's commenced. Get to fightin' or get away!"

Kurt Russell as Wyatt Earp – ***Tombstone (1993)***

Setting:

Earp commands Ike Clanton (Stephen Lang) to fight or leave when Ike comes up to him during the shoot-out at the O.K. Corral with hands raised saying, "Don't shoot. I got no gun."

Movie Trivia:

Stephen Lang, who played Ike Clanton, has appeared in numerous television and film roles, including *Shadow Conspiracy* (1997), which was directed by *Tombstone* (1993) director George P. Cosmatos.

About the Actor:

Kurt Russell spent the early 1970s playing minor league baseball.

"Fuck it."

'Rowdy' Roddy Piper as Nada – ***They Live (1988)***

Setting:

Nada's last words before shooting the transmitter on top of the broadcast building and then being shot by the aliens in a helicopter, who he flips off before dying. By destroying the transmitter, the aliens are revealed.

Movie Trivia:

When the aliens are revealed at the end of the movie, a television show representing *Siskel and Ebert at the Movies* is shown, with the two hosts being aliens. They are heard to say, "All the sex and violence on the screen has gone too far for me. I'm fed up with it. Filmmakers like George Romero and John Carpenter have to show some restraint." This was a little jab by Director John Carpenter at the movie critics.

About the Actor:

Roddy Piper was cast as Nada in *They Live* (1988) after John Carpenter saw him in *WrestleMania III,* where he defeated Adrian Adonis with his famous sleeper hold.

"If I was doing you a favor, I'd let em hang you right now and get it over with. But I don't want you to get off that light. I want you to go on being a big tough gunny. I want you to see what it means to have to live like a big tough gunny. So don't thank me yet pardner. You'll see what I mean. Just wait."

Gregory Peck as Jimmy Ringo – ***The Gunfighter (1950)***

Setting:

Ringo's dying words to Hunt Bromley (Skip Homeier). Bromley shot Ringo in the back, but Ringo told Marshal Mark Strett (Millard Mitchell) to let him go and that he'd drawn first, setting Bromley up to live a life looking over his shoulder, waiting for the same to happen to him.

Movie Trivia:

It's reported that the studio hated Peck's authentic period mustache, and that after the film did not do well at the box office, the head of production at Fox, Spyros P. Skouras, told Peck, "That mustache cost us millions."

About the Actor:

Gregory Peck was nominated for a 1946 Oscar for Best Actor in a Leading Role for his portrayal of Father Francis Chisholm in *The Keys of the Kingdom* (1944). It was his second movie.

"You know, you shouldn't knock Chinese potions. I have something in my pocket right now that'll completely clear up that bruise on your forehead."

*Steven Seagal as Lt. Jack Cole – **The Glimmer Man (1996)***

Setting:

As he is leaving the restaurant, Cole is confronted by security. The guy makes a mistake by asking, "What bruise?" Cole gives him one and then takes out several others too, destroying the restaurant. On the way out, he answers the phone and tells the caller they are closed for renovation for two months.

Movie Trivia:

Keenen Ivory Wayans said of his co-star Seagal, "Steven choreographs his own fight scenes, and he knows what he wants. But I told everyone up front I wasn't going to engage him, I had that in my contract, you know: 'we don't fight.'"

About the Actor:

Steven Seagal's mother was Irish and his father was Jewish.

"I'm fuckface. He's asshole."

Bruce Willis as Joe Hallenbeck – ***The Last Boy Scout (1991)***

Setting:

Hallenbeck's reply when bad guy, Jake (Duke Valenti), tells Jimmy Dix (Damon Wayans), "Shut up, fuckface."

Movie Trivia:

Locations for *The Last Boy Scout* (1991) were primarily centered outdoors in and around Los Angeles.

About the Actor:

Bruce Willis was nominated for a 2001 American Comedy Award for Funniest Male Guest Appearance in a TV Series for his work on *Friends* (2000).

"Mister, you've got a lot to learn about people."

Danny Glover as Malachi 'Mal' Johnson – ***Silverado (1985)***

Setting:

After taking the wagon train's gold back from the thieves, the young man who didn't trust Mal and his three companions shows up and demands the box of gold. Mal's comment comes right before a bullet from one of the thieves hits the young man in the chest. The four heroes return the gold and the body of the killed man.

Movie Trivia:

Shooting for *Silverado* (1985) lasted 96 days, between November 1984 and March 1985.

About the Actor:

Before Danny Glover's movie debut, he appeared in an episode of *B.J. and the Bear* on television in 1979.

"You speaking to me?"

Alan Ladd as Shane – ***Shane (1953)***

Setting:

Chris Calloway (Ben Johnson) walks up to Shane, who is ordering a soda pop for Joey (Brandon De Wilde) at the bar after buying new farm clothes. Chris wants to run off the "sodbuster" and says, "Well, what'll it be? Lemon, strawberry, or lilac, sodbuster?" Shane's reply didn't warn Chris off, but he learns later.

Movie Trivia:

Ben Johnson, who played Calloway in *Shane* (1953), appeared in over 100 films, including roles in *She Wore a Yellow Ribbon* (1949), *The Undefeated* (1969), and *Chisum* (1970) with John Wayne.

About the Actor:

Alan Ladd was born in Hot Springs, Arkansas.

"You ain't forgiven."

Vin Diesel as Dominic Toretto – ***Fast and Furious (2009)***

Setting:

Toretto's comment when he finds Campos (John Ortiz) praying in a Mexican church and shoves a shotgun into his face.

Movie Trivia:

The F-BOMB Camaro, used at the end of the final chase scene through the tunnel, is a duplicate of David Frieberger's real '71 Camaro "F Bomb." Frieberger was the chief editor for *Hot Rod* magazine for years.

About the Actor:

Vin Diesel never knew his biological father.

"Nag, nag, nag."

Kurt Russell as Gabe Cash – ***Tango & Cash (1989)***

Setting:

Cash's reply as he and Tango (Sylvester Stallone) maneuver through electrical wires during their escape from prison. Tango said, "I'm getting real tired of electricity." (They had been tortured with electricity by inmates earlier.)

Movie Trivia:

Patrick Swayze is reported to have been originally cast as Cash, but he dropped out to star in *Road House* (1989).

About the Actor:

Kurt Russell got to say the line that Clint Eastwood repeated several times as Ben Shockley in *The Gauntlet* (1977), "Nag, nag, nag."

"What's the matter, never seen a grown man naked?"

Patrick Swayze as the Nomad – ***Steel Dawn (1987)***

Setting:

Even cool in a bath, the Nomad addresses Damnil (Anthony Zerbe) and his henchmen, who ride up on horses as he bathes in a tub among some rocks. When one gets off his horse to threaten him with a short spear, the Nomad takes it away without getting out of the tub and tells him, "You shouldn't play with sharp objects." Later in the movie, the Nomad gets to say, "I told you not to play with sharp objects," after killing the guy in a kind of joust with wind racers.

Movie Trivia:

Anthony Zerbe, who played bad guy Damnil, played the mad scientist Abner Devereaux, who was defeated by the legendary rock band KISS, in the made for television movie *KISS Meets the Phantom of the Park* (1978).

About the Actor:

Patrick Swayze goes shirtless and had a quick nude scene in *Road House* (1989), which is the only reason many women watch this tough guy flick with their husbands and boyfriends.

"I'd try to explain it to you Claude, but there's some things that just can't be taught."

Tom Berenger as Jonathan Shale – ***The Substitute (1996)***

Setting:

Shale's final words to Principal Claude Rolle (Ernie Hudson), just before killing him. Holding a gun to Shale's head, Rolle stated that Shale was in it for the money, and Shale replied it was never about the money. Rolle then asked if not for money, what else was there.

Movie Trivia:

The Substitute (1996) was written by Roy Frumkes, Rocco Simonelli, and Alan Ormsby.

About the Actor:

Tom Berenger's first wife was Barbara Wilson. They were married from 1976 to 1984, and have two children: Allison (1977) and Patrick (1979).

"Slow is smooth, smooth is fast."

Mark Wahlberg as Bob Lee Swagger – ***Shooter (2007)***

Setting:

Swagger helps Special Agent Nick Memphis (Michael Pena) with his shooting as they prepare to assault the farm house to gather information and find out who Johnson (Danny Glover) is working for.

Movie Trivia:

Author Stephen Hunter appears in *Survival of the Fittest: The Making of "Shooter."* In this, he states that he wanted to write a novel about a sniper after reading a biography of Carlos Hathcock, a Marine sniper.

About the Actor:

Mark Wahlberg was the youngest of nine children to Alma and Donald Wahlberg.

"You're right. My sons were better men."

Mel Gibson as Benjamin Martin – ***The Patriot (2000)***

Setting:

Said to Col. William Tavington (Jason Isaacs) right before killing him. Tavington, who though he had the upper hand, and was preparing to kill Martin, gloated and said, "Kill me before the war is over, will you? It appears you are not the better man."

Movie Trivia:

Jason Isaacs, who played Col. William Tavington, has a long list of movie credits, including his portrayal of Lucius Malfoy in the *Harry Potter* movies.

About the Actor:

Mel Gibson was the first Australian actor to be paid $1,000,000 for a film role.

"Tits to die for, huh?"

Steven Seagal as Casey Ryback – ***Under Siege 2: Dark Territory (1995)***

Setting:

A terrorist yells for a woman to come out of the restroom. She comes out and says, "I broke my bra," and shows him some cleavage. While distracted, Ryback pushes past the woman and kills the terrorist and makes the above comment.

Movie Trivia:

Bad guy Travis Dane in *Under Siege 2 Dark Territory* (1995) is played by Eric Bogosian, who appeared as Captain Danny Ross in *Law & Order: Criminal Intent* (2006 – 2010).

About the Actor:

While living and training in Japan, Steven Seagal earned a 7th degree black belt in Aikido.

"If you have to fire, hold low and squeeze. And put your man down. Because he'd do the same to you. Shoot to kill."

Sean Connery as Jim Malone – ***The Untouchables (1987)***

Setting:

Malone offers some more guidance just before the team takes down a group of bad guys bringing alcohol over the Canadian border. Then, as the Mounties jump the gun, Malone remarks as they get ready to ride down to confront Capone's men, "What the hell! You gotta die of something."

Movie Trivia:

The bridge in the shoot-out scene at the Canadian border was actually the Hardy Bridge, located about thirty miles south of Great Falls, Montana, on the Missouri River.

About the Actor:

Sean Connery enlisted in the Royal Navy when he was sixteen.

"It got complicated."

Eric Roberts as Merle "The Butcher" Henche – ***The Butcher (2007)***

Setting:

Henche's reply to Jackie (Irina Bjorklund) when he gets to the car after killing Doyle (Paul Dillon) and all of his men, including blowing the club apart with a .50 caliber machine gun. She says to him, "That didn't sound like it went well."

Movie Trivia:

Paul Dillon, who played Doyle, has also appeared in the television series *The Shield* (2008) among many others, and movies such as: *Stellina Blue* (2009), *The Blue Hour* (2007), *One Night With You* (2006), and many others.

About the Actor:

Eric Roberts started his acting career at age 5 in a local theater company called the Actors and Writers Workshop founded by his late father, Walter Roberts.

"You're great in the locker room, pal, and your reflexes might die hard, but you're weak when you put your spikes on."

Robert De Niro as Sam – ***Ronin (1998)***

Setting:

At the Coliseum, Sam comes up behind Gregor (Stellan Skarsgard) and puts a gun to his head while Gregor was negotiating a price for the case he stole from Sam and the rest of the group with another party. This is what Sam tells him.

Movie Trivia:

The contents of the case, which the entire movie revolves around, are never revealed or disclosed as to what they are. *Pulp Fiction* (1994) also had a case where the contents were not revealed.

About the Actor:

It's reported that Robert De Niro turned down the role of Jesus in *The Last Temptation of Christ* (1988).

"You've got a big nose, and you're sticking it too far in my business."

Gary Busey as Peter Keyes – ***Predator 2 (1990)***

Setting:

Keyes takes over a crime scene and threatens Lt. Harrigan (Danny Glover) after Harrigan and his team got there first.

Movie Trivia:

The Predator's trophy room contains a skull of a creature that resembles the ones in *Alien* (1979) and *Aliens* (1986).

About the Actor:

Gary Busey was an uncredited extra at the concert in *Wild in the Streets* (1968) that featured Shelly Winters, Hal Holbrook, and Richard Pryor among the stars.

"On any other day, that might seem strange."

*Nicolas Cage as Cameron Poe – **Con Air (1977)***

Setting:

Poe comments on seeing DEA Agent Duncan Molloy's (Colm Meaney) Corvette being pulled through the air behind the aircraft as it takes off from the desert airfield.

Movie Trivia:

DEA Agent Duncan Malloy's (Colm Meaney) key chain has a miniature Star Trek communicator ornament. Meany played Chief Miles O'Brian on *Star Trek: The Next Generation* (1987 – 1994) and *Star Trek: Deep Space Nine* (1993 – 1999).

About the Actor:

Nicolas Cage's first wife was Patricia Arquette (1995 – 2001).

"You can call it the art of fighting without fighting."

Bruce Lee as Lee – ***Enter the Dragon (1973)***

Setting:

Lee's reply to Parsons (Peter Archer) when Parson's asks him, "What's your style?" When Parsons insists that Lee show him this style, Lee has him get into a smaller boat to go to a nearby beach, and then sets him adrift to be pulled behind the larger vessel that is taking them to Han's (Kien Shih) island.

Movie Trivia:

Martial Arts superstar Jackie Chan (in an uncredited role) has his neck dramatically broken by Lee during the big fight scene in Han's underground lab.

About the Actor:

Bruce Lee's gravestone reads, "Founder of Jeet Kune Do." Jeet Kune Do, which means Way of the Intercepting Fist, has become an extremely popular martial art throughout the entire world.

"But a man's got a right to protect his property and his life. And we ain't letting no rancher or his lawman take either."

Robert Duvall as Boss Spearman – ***Open Range (2003)***

Setting:

Spearman's speech to Marshal Poole (James Russo) in the café when Spearman and Waite (Kevin Costner) return to the town to get help for Button (Diego Luna), and to make things right for the death of Mose (Abraham Benrubi) and the shooting of Button by Baxter's (Michael Gambon) men.

Movie Trivia:

Open Range (2003) was filmed in Alberta, Canada.

About the Actor:

Robert Duval played Ned Pepper - the bad guy who was shot by John Wayne at the climax of *True Grit* (1969).

"It's your mistake Rosselini. When you set up my brother, you forgot to kill me."

Patrick Swayze as Truman Gates – ***Next of Kin (1989)***

Setting:

Right before the final confrontation in the cemetery, Joey Rosselini (Adam Baldwin) tells Truman Gates that he's made the same mistake as his brothers, who Rossellini killed. This was Truman Gates' reply.

Movie Trivia:

Ted Levine, who played Captain Leland Stottlemeyer on the popular television show *Monk* (2000 – 2009), is one of the familiar faces appearing in *Next of Kin* (1989). He played Willy Simpson, who was arrested by Truman Gates at the beginning of the film.

About the Actor:

Patrick Swayze was nominated for a Razzie Award for Worst Actor for his roles in *Next of Kin* (1989) and *Road House* (1989), both movies came out the same year.

"The hurt you're feeling now ain't the worst pain. The worst thing is not feeling the hurt anymore."

Tom Berenger as Thomas Beckett – ***Sniper (1993)***

Setting:

Beckett confronts Richard Miller (Billy Zane) after Miller makes his first kill. Miller asks, "After you pull the trigger, when the rush is over, it hurts, doesn't it?"

Movie Trivia:

The weapon used by Richard Miller (Billy Zane) is a Heckler & Koch SR9TC, which is actually a conversion of an HK91, like nearly all of the SR9s seen in Hollywood movies.

About the Actor:

Tom Berenger was considered for the role of Jack Tripper on *Three's Company* (1976 – 1984), a role that ultimately went to John Ritter.

"Yeah, well you can stick your well-laid plan up your well-laid ass."

Samuel L. Jackson as Zeuz Carver – ***Die Hard With a Vengeance (1995)***

Setting:

Bad guy Simon Gruber (Jeremy Irons) asks for the ebony Samaritan who helped McClane (Bruce Willis) when he was wearing the derogatory sign in Harlem, and then tells him, "You interfered with a well-laid plan." Simon hangs up after Carver's response.

Movie Trivia:

Die Hard With a Vengeance (1995) was one of four movies in 1995 with Samual L. Jackson. The movies and characters were Kadar Lewis in *Losing Isaiah* (1995), Calvin Hart in *Kiss of Death* (1995), Zeus Carver in *Die Hard With a Vengeance* (1995), and the voice of Rumbo in *Fluke* (1995).

About the Actor:

One of Samuel L. Jackson's nicknames is "King of Cool."

"We never talked about plan C, asshole. You think it's a dud?"

Kurt Russell as Gabe Cash – ***Tango & Cash (1989)***

Setting:

Cash comments during a fight with the bad guy, Requin (Brion James), when he pulls out a hand grenade, pulls the pin, and drops it in Requin's pants. He then knocks him down a staircase where the grenade explodes. Cash then looks over at Tango (Sylvester Stallone), who just finished off his bad guy, and says, "FUBAR. Big time."

Movie Trivia:

Brion James' initial role as Requin was very small, with only two lines. To make his character stand out, James decided to speak in a cockney accent. Sylvester Stallone loved it and the character Requin was given a bigger role.

About the Actor:

Kurt Russell appeared in the music video and sang in the choir of the song "Voices That Care."

"Hey! Can't we all just get along?"

Jean-Claude Van Damme as Eddie Lomax – ***Desert Heat (1999)***

Setting:

Lomax walks up to the hang out of the Heathens, the Bomb Bay Café, and interrupts the ruckus going on out front with the above. Two women want to leave, but are told they will dance by a thug who starts shooting the ground at their feet, and then makes the café owner dance by shooting at him too. When the man says he doesn't want to get along and slaps one of the girls, Lomax tells him, "You're a very naughty boy." They start something and he kills three with his .45 and then asks, "Who's next?"

Movie Trivia:

Desert Heat (1999), also known as *Inferno* (1999), is a remake of the classic Japanese Kurosawa film *Yojimbo* (1961). To honor the original, near the end of the movie, the tour bus driver, Buddy (Jim Hanks), asks waitress Dottie (Jaime Pressly) out to see the samurai movie *Yojimbo* (1961).

About the Actor:

Jean-Claude Van Damme was an uncredited extra in *Missing in Action* (1984) starring tough guy Chuck Norris.

"There you go, cupcake."

Jason Statham as Chev Chelios – ***Crank 2: High Voltage (2009)***

Setting:

In front of the house where Chelios meets Ria (Ling Bai), he confronts two thugs who pull a gun on him. After sending them running, he says the quote above.

Movie Trivia:

Sadly, David Carradine, who played Poon Dong, passed away 47 days after the release of *Crank 2: High Voltage* (2009) in theaters.

About the Actor:

Jason Statham once worked as a fashion model.

"You mind if we finish this?"

Steve Austin as John Brickner – ***Damage (2009)***

Setting:

During the final fight, when everyone thinks he's dead, or at least out of the fight, Brickner climbs out from under a bunch of barrels, covered with oil, and faces Timmons (Tony Bailey). This is what he says.

Movie Trivia:

Real fighters were hired as jobbers to make the fight sequences more realistic.

About the Actor:

Steve Austin broke the nose of MMA fighter Paul Lazenby while filming a fight scene for *Damage* (2009). Austin was upset with the incident, even though Lazenby insisted it was okay and that it was a complete accident.

"You tell 'em I'm comin' and Hell's comin' with me, you hear? Hell's comin' with me!"

Kurt Russell as Wyatt Earp – ***Tombstone (1993)***

Setting:

Earp lets Ike Clanton (Stephen Lang) go at the train depot with a warning to tell all the cowboys.

Movie Trivia:

When Wyatt Earp is going crazy and yelling at Ike Clanton that hell's comin' with him, Ike is standing in front of a train car #5150, the police code for a crazy person.

About the Actor:

Kurt Russell and Goldie Hawn live on a 72-acre retreat, Home Run Ranch, outside of Aspen, CO.

"But at the end of the day, when all the dust settles, you can't hide from the truth, you son of a bitch."

Mark Wahlberg as Bob Lee Swagger – ***Shooter (2007)***

Setting:

Swagger illustrates in the Attorney General's boardroom that his sniper rifle doesn't shoot because he switched the firing pin as he confronts Colonel Isaac Johnson (Danny Glover). Johnson walks free, but so does Swagger. The next time they meet, Swagger issues the Justice the A.G. couldn't. His justice is not only for Johnson, but for Senator Charles F. Meachum (Ned Beatty) as well.

Movie Trivia:

Ned Beatty, who played Senator Meachum, has a very long list of movie credits, starting with his first role as Bobby Trippe in the film *Deliverance* (1972).

About the Actor:

Mark Wahlberg's first film role was as Pvt. Tommy Lee Haywood in *Renaissance Man* (1994).

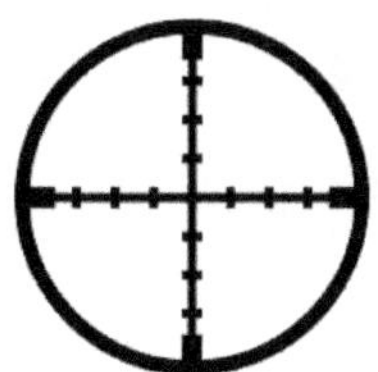

"You know, when you wake up in the morning and look in the mirror, I think you're probably happy, pleased at what you see. And that disturbs me. So, I'm gonna take it on as my responsibility, to make sure that you never get to look in the mirror again."

Steven Seagal as Lt. Jack Cole – ***The Glimmer Man (1996)***

Setting:

Cole to bad guy Donald Cunningham (John M. Jackson) before their final fight near the end of the movie. Cunningham replies, "I woke up happy, I'm going to bed happy, 'cause you're gonna be dead." He was wrong.

Movie Trivia:

The Glimmer Man (1996) was shot entirely on location in the city where its action takes place: Los Angeles, CA.

About the Actor:

Steven Seagal co-produced and co-wrote the song "Snake" performed by Taj Mahal for the movie *The Glimmer Man* (1996).

"You're just not worth killin."

Steven McQueen as Max Sand, aka Nevada Smith – ***Nevada Smith (1966)***

Setting:

Last words Max Sand says before riding off, leaving Tom Fitch (Karl Malden) laying by the creek where Sand shot him, yelling at Sand to finish the job.

Movie Trivia:

Karl Malden, Arthur Kennedy, and Martin Landau played the three killers Max Sand tracks down. Malden and Landau both won Oscars for different films, and Kennedy received five nominations in different films.

About the Actor:

Steve McQueen was 36 years old playing the "kid" Max Sand, and it is uncertain how many years the movie covers.

"No, there's only one left. He's all mine."

Wesley Snipes as John Cutter – ***Passenger 57 (1992)***

Setting:

After knocking out Sabrina Ritchie (Elizabeth Hurley), Cutter turns to leave the cockpit to find terrorist Charles Rane (Bruce Payne), and the pilot asks if he needs help. This is his reply.

Movie Trivia:

Originally, the role played by Wesley Snipes was offered to Sylvester Stallone.

About the Actor:

Wesley Trent Snipes was born on July 31, 1962, in Orlando, Florida.

"Don't try to stop me. I did not come this far to stop now."

Jean-Claude Van Damme as Frank Dux – ***Bloodsport (1988)***

Setting:

Said to Helmer (Norman Burton), Rawlins (Forest Whitaker), and Hong Kong police inspector Chen (Philip Chan) in the alley as they try to stop Dux from going to the kumite finals.

Movie Trivia:

At the end of the movie, the line appears: "This motion picture is based upon the true events in the life of Frank W. Dux." It then says Dux fought 329 matches, and retired undefeated as the World Heavy Weight Full Contact Kumite Champion and listed some of his records. In the credits, Frank Dux is listed as the Fight Coordinator and Special Training for Mr. Van Damme.

About the Actor:

Jean-Claude Van Damme was nominated for a 1989 Razzie Award for Worst New Star for the movie *Bloodsport* (1988).

"What do you say, Jack? Would you like a shot at the title?"

Mel Gibson as Sergeant Martin Riggs – ***Lethal Weapon (1987)***

Setting:

Riggs Challenges Mr. Joshua (Gary Busey) to go hand to hand as he and Murtaugh (Danny Glover) arrest him. Joshua accepts and the two battle it out.

Movie Trivia:

Lethal Weapon (1987) helped reignite Gary Busey's career.

About the Actor:

Mel Gibson was awarded an honorary Doctor of Humane Letters degree from Loyola Marymount University in Los Angeles in May 2003, and gave the commencement address.

"If you touch me again, I'll kill you."

Bruce Willis as Joe Hallenbeck – ***The Last Boy Scout (1991)***

Setting:

Hallenbeck is unconscious in a chair and Chet (Kim Coates) slaps him to wake him up. Hallenbeck catches the next strike and tells Chet he's awake, then asks for a cigarette and light. When he goes to light the cigarette, Chet punches Hallenbeck, who asks for another and tells him the above. When Chet punches Hallenbeck again, he brags, "Two for two." Hallenbeck kills him with one strike and looks down at the body and says, "Told you." He says the line again to Milo (Taylor Negron).

Movie Trivia:

Kim Coats can be seen as Alex 'Tig' Trager on the television series *Sons of Anarchy* (2008 -), but he wasn't killed by Hallenbeck by having his nose driven through his brain as Pablo (Frank Collison) told Milo (Taylor Negron). That's an old urban legend, and the truth is you can't drive the nose bones into the brain, but any forceful blow to the head has the potential to be fatal.

About the Actor:

In 2002, Bruce Willis, on a suggestion from his daughter Tallulah, purchased 12,000 boxes of Girl Scout cookies that were distributed to sailors aboard the USS John F. Kennedy and other troops stationed throughout the Middle East.

"Well, I'm going to start by asking him nicely."

Eric Roberts as Merle "The Butcher" Henche – ***The Butcher (2007)***

Setting:

Henche's reply to Jackie (Irina Bjorklund) when she asks if he has a plan regarding getting the rest of the money from the mobster, Murdock (Robert Davi), that set him up.

Movie Trivia:

Robert Davi, who plays Murdock, has a long line of movie and television credits, including: *Raw Deal* (1986), *Action Jackson* (1988), *Die Hard* (1988), *Licence To Kill* (1989), *Predator 2* (1990), *Showgirls* (1995), *The Dukes* (2007), and many, many more.

About the Actor:

Eric Roberts said after working with Robert Davi, that Davi was one of his favorite three or four actors working on the planet. Roberts says the shoot-out scene with Davi is his favorite shoot-out scene he's ever done.

"Nobody beats me in the kitchen."

Steven Seagal as Casey Ryback – ***Under Siege 2: Dark Territory (1995)***

Setting:

Ryback's comment after disposing of Marcus Penn (Everett McGill) in their climatic fight near the end of the movie. Ryback kills Penn in the train's kitchen, and makes the comment in reference to the joke about him being a cook in the *Under Siege* films. A cook who also happens to be a Navy SEAL.

Movie Trivia:

Everett McGill, who plays Marcus Penn, starred with another tough guy, Clint Eastwood, when he appeared as Major Malcolm A. Powers in *Heartbreak Ridge* (1986).

About the Actor:

One of the charities Steven Seagal supports is "Save a Million Lives." The charity is making an impact on HIV/AIDS in Africa.

"Nobody ever wins a fight."

Patrick Swayze as Dalton – ***Road House (1989)***

Setting:

Dalton's reply to the Doc, Elizabeth Clay (Kelly Lynch), when she asks, "Do you ever win a fight?"

Movie Trivia:

Kathleen Wilhoite, who played Carrie in *Road House* (1989), actually did sing the song "Knock on Wood" with The Jeff Healey Band. She was no stranger to tough guys, since she played Arabella McGee alongside Charles Bronson in *Murphy's Law* (1986).

About the Actor:

Patrick Swayze's co-star in the hit *Ghost* (1990), Demi Moore, released this statement upon hearing of Swayze's death, "Patrick you are loved by so many and your light will forever shine in all of our lives, in the words of Sam to Molly, 'It's amazing Molly. The love inside, you take it with you.' I will miss you. Demi."

"I beg to differ, sir. We started a game we never got to finish. Play for blood, remember?"

Val Kilmer as Doc Holliday – ***Tombstone (1993)***

Setting:

Holliday meets Johnny Ringo (Michael Biehn) when Ringo is expecting Wyatt Earp (Kurt Russell). After Holliday greets him with, "I'm your Huckleberry," Ringo looks surprised. Holliday says, "Why, Johnny Ringo, you look like somebody just walked over your grave." Ringo replies, "Fight's not with you, Holliday." Holliday returns with the line above. Ringo says, "I was just foolin' about." Holliday says, "I wasn't."

Movie Trivia:

It's reported that the role of Johnny Ringo was originally offered to Mickey Rourke, but he turned it down.

About the Actor:

Val Kilmer shares something with Adam West. Both actors have played Doc Holliday and Batman.

"I've made 'em before."

Tom Laughlin as Billy Jack – ***Billy Jack (1971)***

Setting:

Billy's reply to Posner (Bert Freed) after he tells Posner to have his men drop their guns and leave quietly, and Posner tells him, "You're making a mistake."

Movie Trivia:

Tom Laughlin first had the idea for the character Billy Jack in 1953, after witnessing discrimination toward Native American's in a small South Dakota town. He poured out his anger over the racism in his motel room and came up with the first draft of his screenplay. Seventeen years later, he finally made the movie *Billy Jack* (1971).

About the Actor:

Tom Laughlin played football at Wisconsin's Marquette University.

"The bill for helping the Indian girl included kicked in ribs, a broken nose, one eye mashed up pretty good, but all I needed was a gun. And some time to heal."

Bruce Willis as John Smith – ***Last Man Standing (1996)***

Setting:

Smith narrates as he is taken to the abandoned church to heal.

Movie Trivia:

Mob boss Doyle is played by David Patrick Kelly, who got his start in another Walter Hill film, *The Warriors* (1979). Kelly played Luther, who had the famous line, "Warriors, come out to play…"

About the Actor:

Tough guy Bruce Willis was the voice of the baby "Mikey" in *Look Who's Talking* (1989) and *Look Who's Talking Too* (1990).

"We're different you and I. Your spirit is more calm and pacific in you than in any person I've ever known. And mine has been in a violent rage since the day that I was born. And you know something, I didn't really want it that way."

Tom Laughlin as Billy Jack – ***Billy Jack (1971)***

Setting:

Billy and Jean (Delores Taylor) talk in the barn just before Billy gives himself up to the police outside.

Movie Trivia:

Delores Taylor, who plays Jean Roberts, was nominated for a 1972 Golden Globe for Most Promising Newcomer – Female for *Billy Jack* (1971).

About the Actor:

The official website for Tom Laughlin and Delores Taylor is www.billyjack.com.

"Don't bet on it."

Eric Roberts as Alexander Grady – ***Best of the Best 2 (1993)***

Setting:

Tommy Lee (Phillip Rhee) defeats Brakus (Ralf Moeller) and announces that the Coliseum is closed. Manager Weldon (Wayne Newton) pleads with Tommy and Alex that they need him to make a lot of money. Alex hits Weldon in the nose with an elbow and continues to walk off. Weldon says he'll be back, and Alex's final comment is above as he turns out the lights of the Coliseum and credits roll.

Movie Trivia:

Phillip Rhee's brother, Simon Rhee, reprises his role as Dae Han from the first film, *Best of the Best* (1989).

About the Actor:

Eric Roberts appeared in six episodes of the popular television series *Heroes* (2007 – 2008) as Thompson.

"Jesus, Richie."

Viggo Mortensen as Tom Stall, aka Joey Cusack – ***A History of Violence (2005)***

Setting:

Said right after shooting his brother Richie Cusack (William Hurt) who was trying to kill him. Right before being shot, Richie said, "Jesus, Joey." These were the last spoken words of the movie. In the scenes where Stall gets rid of the gun and when he returns home to his family, not a word is spoken.

Movie Trivia:

William Hurt was nominated for an Oscar for Best Performance by an Actor in a Supporting Role, even though he only appeared in the final scene and filmed his role in five days.

About the Actor:

The height of Viggo Peter Mortensen Jr. is listed as 5'11" (1.80m).

"Pennington smacked the crap out of Bo and his old man, and I let him."

Tom Selleck as Jesse Stone – ***Stone Cold (2005)***

Setting:

Over drinks, attorney Rita Fiore (Mimi Rogers) asks, off the record, what really happened to Bo (Shawn Roberts) and his father. Besides the above, Stone tells her he'd testify that, "Bo attacked Candace's (Alexis Dziena) dad who responded in self-defense. Then Joe Marino (Tony De Santis) jumped in and Chuck (Ralph Small) had to defend himself from both of them."

Movie Trivia:

The character Rita Fiore originated in Robert B. Parker's *Spencer* series. The character was portrayed by Carolyn McCormick in the series *Spencer: For Hire* (1985), and by Laila Robins in *Spencer: Small Vices* (1999).

About the Actor:

Tom Selleck is a member of the Sigma Chi Fraternity.

"Everybody walks away breathing, everybody wins."

Tommy Lee Jones as Chief Deputy Marshal Samuel Gerard – ***U.S. Marshals (1998)***

Setting:

Gerard catches up with fugitive Mark J. Sheridan (Wesley Snipes) who is holding a gun against Special Agent John Royce's (Robert Downey Jr.) neck. Gerard also tells him, "Drop the gun pal. It's been a long day for everybody. Let's end it on a positive note." Royce replies, "For me, or for you?"

Movie Trivia:

The marshals' first encounter with their fugitive was shot at Reelfoot Lake in northwest Tennessee. The same location was used for the films *Raintree Country* (1957), staring Elizabeth Taylor, and the Oscar-winning classic *In the Heat of the Night* (1967).

About the Actor:

Tommy Lee Jones roomed with future Vice President Al Gore when they were both attending Harvard University.

"I changed my mind."

Alan Ladd as Shane – ***Shane (1953)***

Setting:

After Shane knocks out Joe Starrett and prepares to go face Rufus Ryker (Emile Meyer) and Jack Wilson (Jack Palance), Marian Starrett (Jean Arthur) says to him, "Shane, wait. You were through with gunfighting." This was his simple answer.

Movie Trivia:

Shane (1953) was Jean Arthur's last movie role. She appeared in nearly 100 movies, including *Mr. Smith Goes To Washington* (1939), *The Devil and Miss Jones* (1941), and *A Foreign Affair* (1948).

About the Actor:

In 1953, Alan Ladd appeared in three other movies besides *Shane* (1953). They were *Botany Boy* (1953), *Desert Legion* (1953), and *Paratrooper* (1953).

"Sit your ass down, Clarence."

Samuel L. Jackson as Neville Flynn – ***Snakes on a Plane (2006)***

Setting:

Agent Flynn takes his gun back from rapper Three G's (Flex Alexander) and tells him to sit so he can go back to saving the plane.

Movie Trivia:

Flight attendant Claire Miller was played by Julianna Margulies, who is known for her roles as nurse Carol Hathaway on the hit television series *ER* (1994 – 2009), and attorney Alicia Florrick in *The Good Wife* (2009 -).

About the Actor:

Samuel L. Jackson played Stan in *Together for Days* (1972), one of his earliest roles.

"I told you to come alone. I guess that was too complicated. So try this, I'm gone."

Matt Damon as Jason Bourne – ***The Bourne Identity (2002)***

Setting:

Bourne calls Conklin (Chris Cooper) as he waits for him on the bridge for their face-to-face meeting, and tells him this.

Movie Trivia:

The characters played by Brian Cox (Ward Abbott) and Chris Cooper (Conklin) are never referred to by name until the end credits.

About the Actor:

Matt Damon's older brother, Kyle, is a sculptor.

"What I really hate, is a pussy with a gun in his hand."

Clive Owen as Smith – ***Shoot 'Em Up (2007)***

Setting:

Smith's words, after finally killing the main bad guy Hertz (Paul Giamatti), in the final shootout between the two.

Movie Trivia:

Shoot 'Em Up (2007) was written and directed by Michael Davis.

About the Actor:

Clive Owen married Sarah-Jane Fenton in 1995, and they have two children.

"Well, ya see, I'm not saying that I've been everywhere and I done everything, but I do know it's a pretty amazing planet we live on here, and a man would have to be some kind of fool to think we're all alone in this universe."

Kurt Russell as Jack Burton – ***Big Trouble in Little China (1986)***

Setting:

Burton driving his truck at the beginning of the movie giving out advice over the CB Radio.

Movie Trivia:

Big Trouble in Little China (1986) was directed by John Carpenter, who also directed *Halloween* (1978) and *They Live* (1988) among others.

About the Actor:

Kurt Russell and John Carpenter are good friends and *Big Trouble in Little China* (1986) was the fourth John Carpenter movie Russell starred in. The first three were: *Elvis* (1979), *Escape from New York* (1981), and *The Thing* (1982). Ten years after *Big Trouble in Little China* (1986), they did their fifth film together, *Escape from L.A.* (1996).

"Never stop. Never stop fighting till the fight is done."

Kevin Costner as Eliot Ness – ***The Untouchables (1987)***

Setting:

Eliot Ness to Al Capone (Robert De Niro) in the final courtroom scene.

Movie Trivia:

The real Eliot Ness and Al Capone never came face to face during their battles. It made a good movie moment though.

About the Actor:

Kevin Costner was helped by Albert H. Wolff, the last survivor of the real-life Untouchables, for his portrayal of Eliot Ness.

"Is that the best you got, boy? If that's the best you got, I'm just gonna have to kill you."

Steven Seagal as Lt. Jack Cole – ***The Glimmer Man (1996)***

Setting:

Cole to bad guy Donald Cunningham (John M. Jackson) during their final fight, just before killing him. He then looks at the body and says, "You don't look like you're gonna be wakin' up happy now."

Movie Trivia:

The song "Bulletproof," during the ending credits, was performed by The Jeff Healey Band. The late Jeff Healey appeared in the tough guy movie *Road House* (1989).

About the Actor:

Steven Seagal co-wrote the song "Bulletproof" performed by The Jeff Healey Band for the movie *The Glimmer Man* (1996).

"Be prepared, son. That's my motto. Be prepared."

Bruce Willis as Joe Hallenbeck – ***The Last Boy Scout (1991)***

Setting:

Last lines of the movie after Hallenbeck takes Jimmy Dix (Damon Wayans) on as a partner and tells him, "Water's wet, the sky is blue, and old Satan Claus, Jimmy, he's out there, and he's just getting stronger." Dix then asks, "So, what do we do about that?"

Movie Trivia:

It's reported that composer Michael Kamen hated the film when he first saw it, but provided the score because of his friendships with Bruce Willis and Joel Silver.

About the Actor:

In 2005, Bruce Willis stated that he wanted to "make a pro-war film in which American soldiers will be depicted as brave fighters for freedom and democracy."

"Ain't just gunplay. You know that, Everett. You gotta think about men too."

Ed Harris as Virgil Cole – ***Appaloosa (2008)***

Setting:

Cole and Everett Hitch (Viggo Mortensen) discuss the death of Jack Bell (Robert Jauregui, as Bobby Jauregui), and that it takes more than just being fast with a gun to be a lawman.

Movie Trivia:

Robert Jauregui, who had the short part as Jack Bell, has only appeared as an actor in one other film. He played Cullen in *Bonanza: The Next Generation* (1988). However, he has a long list of credits for his stunt work.

About the Actor:

Ed Harris won a Festival Prize at the 2008 Boston Film Festival for Best Screenplay Adaptation for *Appaloosa* (2008).

"You talk too much."

Patrick Swayze as the Nomad – ***Steel Dawn (1987)***

Setting:

The Nomad's reply during the final fight when the hired killer, Sho (Christopher Neame), states, "You're the best competition I've ever had. But no one is better than me."

Movie Trivia:

Christopher Neame, who played Sho, appeared in both *Licence to Kill* (1989) and *Ghostbusters II* (1989) in the same year.

About the Actor:

Patrick Swayze owned a five-acre ranch called Rancho Bizarro outside of Los Angeles, California.

"I pick up guns, bad things happen to people. I don't like that."

Dwayne "The Rock" Johnson as Beck – ***The Rundown (2003)***

Setting:

Beck explains to Travis Walker (Seann William Scott) why he doesn't use guns. Travis asks, "What kind of things?" Beck replies, "Very bad things, Travis."

Movie Trivia:

The Rundown (2003) was directed by Peter Berg. The first film Berg directed was *Very Bad Things* (1998).

About the Actor:

Dwayne Johnson's father, Rocky Johnson, was also a wrestler. So were his grandfather, three uncles, and six cousins (one adopted).

"Yoshida, go ahead, use your gun. You don't have the honor to fight like a man."

Dolph Lundgren as Sgt. Chris Kenner – ***Showdown In Little Tokyo (1991)***

Setting:

Kenner calls out to yakuza Funekei Yoshida (Cary-Hiroyuki Tagawa), setting up the final sword fight between the two.

Movie Trivia:

Tia Carrere, who played Minako Okeya, appeared with other tough guys Sean Connery in *Rising Sun* (1993) and Arnold Schwarzenegger in *True Lies* (1994). She proved to be tough herself in the television series *Relic Hunter* (1999 – 2002).

About the Actor:

Dolph Lundgren received a master's degree in chemical engineering from the University of Sydney, New South Wales, Australia.

"Imagine the future, Chains, 'cause you're not in it."

Brian Bosworth as Joe Huff/John Stone – ***Stone Cold (1991)***

Setting:

After the final fight between Huff and gang leader Chains (Lance Henriksen), Huff holds a revolver up to Chains' head and says this line. He pulls the trigger and the firearm goes click, it was empty. Huff lets Chains fall down the stairs to be arrested by the FBI. However, when Chains grabs a gun from a police officer, FBI Agent Lance (Sam McMurray) shoots him and tells Huff, "Hey, partner. It's time to turn it on."

Movie Trivia:

The movie never provides FBI Agent Lance's full name. He is just referred to as Lance in the movie and in the credits.

About the Actor:

On the first page of his book, *The Boz: Confessions of a Modern Anti-Hero*, Brian Bosworth writes, "Pain and blood let you know you're playing serious football."

"I'm gonna show you God does exist."

Nicolas Cage as Cameron Poe – ***Con Air (1997)***

Setting:

Poe's reply to Mike 'Baby-O' O'Dell (Mykelti Williamson). O'Dell is lying in the aircraft thinking he won't make it after being shot, and tells Poe, "All I can think about is, like, there ain't no God. That He don't exist. Hey, where you goin'?"

Movie Trivia:

According to the letter from Poe's daughter, Poe's flight was July 14th. In France, July 14th is a National Holiday, Bastille Day, commemorating the storming of the Bastille and marking the beginning of the French Revolution. The Bastille was a prison that held seven inmates.

About the Actor:

Nicolas Cage won an Oscar for Best Actor in a Leading Role for his role as Ben Sanderson in *Leaving Las Vegas* (1995).

"No Way You Live. No Way."

Danny Glover as Sergeant Roger Murtaugh – ***Lethal Weapon (1987)***

Setting:

Murtaugh's comment before putting a bullet into the head of General Peter McAllister's (Mitch Ryan) driver, resulting in the car being hit by a bus and a hand grenade blowing McAllister to kingdom come, or as Murtaugh puts it to Mr. Joshua (Gary Busey) later, "Looking for your general friend? He's barbecuing his nuts on Hollywood Boulevard."

Movie Trivia:

The song "Lethal Weapon" was performed by Honeymoon Suite.

About the Actor:

Danny Glover's movie debut was as an inmate in the movie *Escape From Alcatraz* (1979) starring Clint Eastwood.

"John, what the fuck are you doing out on the wing of this plane?"

Bruce Willis as Lt. John McClane – ***Die Hard 2 Die Harder (1990)***

Setting:

McClane talks to himself right after he jumps from the news helicopter to the wing of a moving plane. The plane is controlled by terrorists who are preparing to take off.

Movie Trivia:

Some of the movie was filmed at the old Stapleton Airport in Denver, Colorado. Due to an unseasonably lack of snow, a fair amount of snow had to be created artificially.

About the Actor:

Bruce Willis claims drunken guys always try to start fights with him because of his tough guy persona.

"Hay? Hay is for horses. What is Japan bashing? What does it mean? All animals are created equal except the Japanese? You stupid little shit, fuck off."

Sean Connery as Capt. John Connor – ***Rising Sun (1993)***

Setting:

As Capt. Connor gets into his car, he hits Willy 'The Weasel' Wilhelm (Steve Buscemi) with his door, prompting a surprised, "hey." Connor not only replies to the "hey" exclamation, but also to the Weasel's question, "Captain Connor, do you have any comment on the charge of Japan bashing leveled against you in tonight's paper?"

Movie Trivia:

One of the changes in adapting Michael Crichton's novel for the film was changing Caucasian Peter Smith to African-American Webster (Webb) Smith, the character played by Wesley Snipes.

About the Actor:

Steven Spielberg once said, "There are seven genuine movie stars in the world today, and Sean is one of them."

"It was all personal to me."

Liam Neeson as Bryan Mills – ***Taken (2008, US release 2009)***

Setting:

Reply to bad guy St. Clair's (Gerard Watkins) statement, "Please understand, it was all business. It wasn't personal," just before killing him.

Movie Trivia:

The tag line for *Taken* (2008, US Release 2009) is "They Took His Daughter. He'll Take Their Lives."

About the Actor:

On *Late Night With Jimmy Fallon* (Jan. 16, 2012), Liam Neeson said when they were filming *Taken* (2008, US release 2009), he thought it would go straight to video.

"Relax, I'm a doctor."

Jude Law as Dr. John Watson – ***Sherlock Holmes (2009)***

Setting:

Watson's comment to the large Dredger (Robert Maillet) as he struggles to restrain him to give Sherlock Holmes (Robert Downey Jr.) time to go and confront Lord Blackwood (Mark Strong). Finally, Dredger goes unconscious.

Movie Trivia:

Reportedly, Rachel McAdams, Jude Law, and Robert Downey Jr. did most of their own stunts.

About the Actor:

David Jude Law was born on December 29, 1972, in Lewisham, London, England.

"Enough is enough! I have had it with these motherfucking snakes on this motherfucking plane!"

Samuel L. Jackson as Neville Flynn – ***Snakes on a Plane (2006)***

Setting:

Agent Flynn is fed up with the snakes on the plane and finishes his tirade with, "Everybody strap in. I'm about to open some fucking windows." He then shoots out some windows of the plane and the snakes are sucked outside.

Movie Trivia:

For network television this quote was changed to "Enough is enough! I have had it with these monkey fighting snakes on this Monday to Friday plane!"

About the Actor:

Samuel Jackson joked with Conan O'Brien on *The Tonight Show* (July 8, 2009) regarding the "monkey fighting snakes" replacement, and also said he used, "Marilyn Farmer" as a replacement for his catch phrase at times.

"Yeah, it's laundry day."

'Bruce Willis as John McClane – ***Die Hard With a Vengeance (1995)***

Setting:

McClane goes into the federal building looking pretty ragged and introduces himself to a bad guy in a Federal Reserve uniform. This was his reply when the man asked, "Are you all right?"

Movie Trivia:

It's reported that the reply, "Yeah, it's laundry day" was ad-libbed by Bruce Willis.

About the Actor:

While Bruce Willis was still in his teens, his parents separated in 1972.

"Well, I haven't killed you yet."

Mel Gibson as Sergeant Martin Riggs – ***Lethal Weapon (1987)***

Setting:

Riggs replies to Murtaugh's (Danny Glover) question, "You ever met anybody you didn't kill?" as they climb out of a swimming pool they jumped into to try and retrieve a bad guy Riggs shot.

Movie Trivia:

The extended Director's Cut version of *Lethal Weapon* (1987) has over seven minutes of previously unavailable scenes.

About the Actor:

Mel Gibson's salary for *Summer City* (1977) was $400 (Australian).

"Welcome to the human race."

Kurt Russell as Snake Plissken – ***Escape From L.A. (1996)***

Setting:

Plissken's final words after shutting down all the machinery in the world, lighting a cigarette, and blowing out the match.

Movie Trivia:

It was easy to recognize Pam Grier as Hershe Las Palmas and Peter Fonda as Pipeline, but you have to watch closer to recognize *Revenge of the Nerds* (1984) star Robert Carradine as the skinhead Plissken shoots when the skinhead attempts to throw a knife at Plissken's back.

About the Actor:

Kurt Russell's son, Wyatt Russell, plays an orphan boy in *Escape From L.A.* (1996).

"No questions. No answers. That's the business we're in. You accept it and move on. Maybe that's lesson number three."

Jean Reno as Vincent – ***Ronin (1998)***

Setting:

Final lines, thought by Vincent, as he walks off after saying "goodbye" to Sam (Robert De Niro). In that exchange, he asked Sam what was in the case, and Sam replied he didn't remember. That was lesson two from earlier in the movie.

Movie Trivia:

Many weapons are used in *Ronin* (1998), however, Vincent (Jean Reno) only uses one gun throughout the movie, a Beretta 92FS.

About the Actor:

Jean Reno's birth name was Juan Moreno y Herrera Jimenez and he was born on July 30, 1948, in Casablanca, Morocco.

"Somehow, I don't think he's gonna get the chance."

Steven Seagal as John Hatcher – ***Marked For Death (1990)***

Setting:

Hatcher gets to his sister Melissa's (Elizabeth Gracen) house just in time to save her from Screwface (Basil Wallace). This was his reply when Melissa told him, "He said he'd be back. He said he'd kill us both."

Movie Trivia:

The villain Screwface (Basil Wallace) was named after a Bob Marley song.

About the Actor:

Steven Seagal was listed as a Producer for *Marked For Death* (1990).

"Give me the biggest guy in the world, you smash his knee, he'll drop like a stone."

Patrick Swayze as Dalton – ***Road House (1989)***

Setting:

Dalton provides some words of wisdom to one of the bouncers after a fight outside the Double Deuce.

Movie Trivia:

Benny "the Jet" Urquidez used Michael Jackson's "Thriller" to help Patrick Swayze get rhythm when practicing Urquidez's kickboxing style for the fight scenes in *Road House* (1989).

About the Actor:

Patrick Swayze blew out his knee during a high school football game on Halloween night, 1970. It was an event that changed his life forever.

"Now, let's try that again. Don't make me kill you, tough guy."

*Kurt Russell as Jack Burton – **Big Trouble in Little China (1986)***

Setting:

Burton, escaping from David Lo Pan's (James Hong) room with skeletons, grabs Thunder (Carter Wong), holds a knife to his neck, and tells him the above. This is his second attempt, the first time he grabbed Thunder and said, "You make one move…" and Thunder threw him across the room into a wall.

Movie Trivia:

Carter Wong, who plays Thunder, was a martial arts instructor for the Royal Hong Kong Police Department.

About the Actor:

John Carpenter says that Kurt Russell was Disney trained and got a real good work ethic from that, and that he is dedicated to the craft of acting.

"Of course he's willing to die. You think we do this because we're scared to die?"

Ed Harris as Virgil Cole – ***Appaloosa (2008)***

Setting:

Cole faces a mob outside the jail while Hitch (Viggo Mortensen) keeps a shotgun on Randall Bragg (Jeremy Irons) inside. After Cole says he's willing to die to keep the mob from taking Bragg, the leader, Vince (Timothy V. Murphy), yells inside, "Hitch, you willing to die too?" Cole answers for Hitch, and then asks if Vince is afraid to die. When Vince replies he ain't afraid, Cole tells him, "Good, because you go first."

Movie Trivia:

Timothy V. Murphy, who played Vince, was seen the year before as Seth in *National Treasure 2: Book of Secrets* (2007).

About the Actor:

Ed Harris' father, Bob Harris, plays Judge Elias Callison in *Appaloosa* (2008).

"Like you said, there's a point I won't go beyond."

John Saxon as Roper – ***Enter the Dragon (1973)***

Setting:

Han (Kien Shih) asks Roper, "Would you be good enough to participate in this morning's edification?" Han instructs Roper to fight/kill Lee (Bruce Lee), in which Roper refuses with the above line. Han then pits Roper against Bolo (Bolo Yeung/Yang Sze). Roper kills Bolo and then fights a legion of Han's men alongside Lee.

Movie Trivia:

It's reported that biker movie legend William Smith was supposed to play Roper but was unavailable at the time of the shoot.

About the Actor:

John Saxon's birth name was Carmine Orrico, and he was born on August 5th, 1935, in Brooklyn, New York.

"Well, you may not know this, but there's things that gnaw on a man worse than dying."

Kevin Costner as Charley Waite – ***Open Range (2003)***

Setting:

Waite's comment to men in the saloon after he tells them they could do something about the crooked Baxter (Michael Gambon) who runs the town, and one man replies that he didn't raise his boys just to see them killed.

Movie Trivia:

Open Range (2003) was directed and co-produced by Kevin Costner.

About the Actor:

Kevin Costner had three children, Annie, Lily, and Joe with his first wife Cindy Silva. Costner and Silva divorced in 1994 after 16 years of marriage.

"The chain in those handcuffs is high tensile steel. It'll take you ten minutes to hack through it with this. Now, if you're lucky, you can hack through your ankle in five minutes. Go."

Mel Gibson as Max Rockatansky – ***Mad Max (1979)***

Setting:

Max handcuffs Johnny the Boy (Tim Burns) to the wreckage of a crashed vehicle, sets a lighter and gas to explode, and says the above as he drops a hacksaw next to Johnny the Boy. Max drives off and we see an explosion behind him. The movie ends.

Movie Trivia:

It is reported that Director George Miller, who was a physician, raised money to make *Mad Max* (1979) by working as an Emergency Room Doctor.

About the Actor:

Mel Gibson is the only actor wearing real leathers in *Mad Max* (1979). The other police officers were actually wearing cheaper vinyl costumes due to the budget.

"There were going to be a lot more wooden boxes in Smiley's window. But what the hell, everybody ends up dead. Just a matter of when."

Bruce Willis as John Smith – ***Last Man Standing (1996)***

Setting:

Smith narrates just before going in to kill more bad guys in a shoot-out after healing at the church.

Movie Trivia:

Smith passes a poster of Wild Bill Hickok on his way to a shoot-out (just before the quote on this page). Director Walter Hill also directed *Wild Bill* (1995).

About the Actor:

Bruce Willis was his high school student council president.

"You are not my father. And the breath I take after I kill you will be the first breath of my life."

Rain as Raizo – ***Ninja Assassin (2009)***

Setting:

Raizo addresses Ozunu (Sho Kosugi) before their final battle.

Movie Trivia:

Korean pop star Rain had no martial arts experience prior to shooting *Ninja Assassin* (2009). He trained extensively for six months in martial arts and weapons handling to prepare for the film. His training also included weights and cardio workouts with personal trainers.

About the Actor:

Rain was born in Seoul, South Korea, on June 25, 1982, with the birth name Jeong Ji-hoon.

"Keep the faith, Stranix."

Steven Seagal as Casey Ryback – ***Under Siege (1992)***

Setting:

Ryback's comment after killing William Stranix (Tommy Lee Jones). Before their fight, Ryback told Stranix the two of them were alike, they were the same. Stranix replied, "No, no, no. There's a difference, my man. You have faith. I don't."

Movie Trivia:

Under Siege (1992) is the third Steven Seagal movie Tom Muzila appeared in. Muzila is a bodyguard and an accomplished martial artist who has authored books, DVDs, and audio programs on karate.

About the Actor:

Steven Seagal is a proficient blues artist, and has honed his guitar skills playing his music with some of the greatest blues legends around, including BB King, Bo Diddley, John Lee Hooker, and his greatest influence: the late Clarence "Gatemouth" Brown.

"Isn't that just like a wop? Brings a knife to a gunfight."

Sean Connery as Jim Malone – ***The Untouchables (1987)***

Setting:

Malone confronts a criminal in his apartment. As the man sneaks up on him with a knife, Malone turns around with a sawed off shotgun. Unfortunately for Malone, Frank Nitti (Billy Drago) was waiting outside with a Tommy Gun.

Movie Trivia:

Billy Drago, who played Frank Nitti, next appeared in the Chuck Norris movie *Hero and the Terror* (1988) as Dr. Highwater.

About the Actor:

Sean Connery has two tattoos. One reads "Mum and Dad," and the other says "Scotland Forever."

"You are such an asshole."

Patrick Swayze as Dalton – ***Road House (1989)***

Setting:

Dalton's reply at the beginning of the fight against Jimmy (Marshall Teague) near the lake when Jimmy says, "Prepare to die." Ever the tough guy, during the fight when Jimmy says, "Damn, boy. I thought you were good." Dalton replies, "Go fuck yourself."

Movie Trivia:

Marshall Teague, who played Jimmy in *Road House* (1989), has appeared in numerous movies and television shows, including: *The A Team* (1985); *MacGyver* (1989 - 1990); *Star Trek Deep Space Nine* (1995); *Renegade* (1995 – 1996); *The Rock* (1996); *Star Trek: Voyager* (1997); *Babylon 5* (1994 – 1998); *Pensacola: Wings of Gold* (1998 – 2000); *Walker, Texas Ranger* (1993 – 2001); *U.S. Seals II* (2001), and *Friday Night Lights* (2010 – 2011). Plus a whole lot more.

About the Actor:

Patrick Swayze performed the song "Raising Heaven (in Hell) Tonight" on the *Road House* (1989) soundtrack.

"I'm too tired. Maybe later."

Kurt Russell as Snake Plissken – ***Escape From New York (1981)***

Setting:

Plissken's reply to Hauk (Lee Van Cleef) when asked, "You gonna kill me now, Snake?" Hauk goes on to offer another deal to Snake, and in reply Snake says, "The name's Plissken." He then walks away unraveling the cassette tape the President (Donald Pleasence) was going to play for the summit.

Movie Trivia:

The Girl in Chock Full O'Nuts was played by Season Hubley, who, at the time, was married to Kurt Russell.

About the Actor:

Kurt Russell was married to Season Hubley from 1979 to 1983. They had one child, Boston Russell.

"O.K., just a few words. Fuck off."

*Bruce Willis as Lt. John McClane – **Die Hard 2 Die Harder (1990)***

Setting:

In their second meeting, McClane and reporter Sam Coleman (Sheila McCarthy) are in an elevator leaving the tower. McClane stops the elevator so he can exit through the trap door in the roof. She asks, "Big drug dealer on his way to prison, gunfight at airport, every controller in the coffee shot getting beeped and hauling ass, and you rocking the boat. Connection? Come on McClane. Just a few words." This is his reply.

Movie Trivia:

John McTiernan, who directed the first and third *Die Hard* films, had planned to direct this film, but couldn't because of his commitment to directing *The Hunt for Red October* (1990).

About the Actor:

It's reported that Bruce Willis was one of 3,000 hopefuls that auditioned for the TV series *Moonlighting* (1985 – 1989).

"That gun work?" ("Yeah" - Larkin) "Then shoot that piece of shit!"

Nicolas Cage as Cameron Poe – ***Con Air (1997)***

Setting:

Poe's conversation with U.S. Marshal Vince Larkin (John Cusack) as they both chase a fire truck riding motorcycles. The convict needing shot is Nathan 'Diamond Dog' Jones (Ving Rhames) who is shooting at them.

Movie Trivia:

Con Air (1997) opened in theaters in the United Sates and other countries on June 6, 1997.

About the Actor:

Nicolas Cage earned $5000.00 for his role in *Valley Girl* (1983), and earned $20 million for *National Treasure* (2004).

"It's not the years, honey, it's the mileage."

Harrison Ford as Indiana Jones – ***Raiders of the Lost Ark (1981)***

Setting:

After taking off his shirt on the ship, Marion (Karen Allen) tells Indy, "You're not the man I knew ten years ago." This was his reply.

Movie Trivia:

Raiders of the Lost Ark (1981) won four Oscars: Best Art Direction-Set-Direction, Norman Reynolds, Leslie Dilley, Michael Ford; Best Effects – Visual Effects, Richard Edlund, Kit West, Bruce Nicholson, Joe Johnston; Best Film Editing, Michael Kahn; and Best Sound, Bill Varney, Steve Maslow, Gregg Landaker, Roy Charman.

About the Actor:

Harrison Ford ad-libbed the line, "It's not the years, honey, it's the mileage."

"That gal's got entirely too many brains to have an ass like that."

Sam Elliot as Wade Garrett – ***Road House (1989)***

Setting:

Garrett comments to Dalton (Patrick Swayze) as he watches Elizabeth Clay (Kelly Lynch) walk off to the ladies room.

Movie Trivia:

The band playing at the start of the movie is the band Cruzados. After the band disbanded, the singer Tito Larriva formed the band Tito and Tarantula, which is thc band that plays at the Titty Twister in the movie *From Dusk Till Dawn* (1996).

About the Actor:

Sam Elliot is an alumnus of Clark College in Vancouver, WA.

"Hey, Carmine, let me ask you something. What sets off the metal detectors first – the lead in your ass or the shit in your brains? Fat fuck."

Bruce Willis as Lt. John McClane – ***Die Hard 2 Die Harder (1990)***

Setting:

Said to Capt. Carmine Larenzo (Dennis Franz), as McClane is leaving his office after Larenzo dismisses McClane's warning and says he has other things to worry about.

Movie Trivia:

Dennis Franz, who played Capt. Carmine Larenzo, has played many police officers on screen, including the character Andy Sipowicz in the popular long running television hit *NYPD Blue* (1993 – 2005).

About the Actor:

Early on, Bruce Willis performed regularly on the harmonica in a blues ensemble called the Loose Goose.

"You fuck with my family, you die."

Steven Seagal as John Hatcher – ***Marked For Death (1990)***

Setting:

Said to one of the Jamaican Posse members during the fight in the jewelry store. Hatcher then walks over to Max (Keith David), who just knocked a guy out by striking him with his shotgun, and says, "Now we're talking serious fun, man." Max replies, "Abso-fucking-lutely."

Movie Trivia:

Marked For Death (1990) was directed by Dwight H. Little, who also directed *Halloween 4: The Return of Michael Myers* (1988), *Murder at 1600* (1997), and *Free Willy 2: The Adventure Home* (1995) among many others.

About the Actor:

The song "John Crow" in the movie *Marked For Death* (1990) was written by Jimmy Cliff and Steven Seagal and performed by Jimmy Cliff, Steven Seagal, and The Oneness Band. This was the first singing appearance by Steven Seagal.

"I'm going outside. You don't come out, I'll come back in and kill you."

Viggo Mortensen as Everett Hitch – ***Appaloosa (2008)***

Setting:

Hitch calls Randall Brag (Jeremy Irons) out, right after saying to him, "You're a lying, back-shooting, cowardly son-of-a-bitch."

Movie Trivia:

Jeremy Irons, who plays Randall Bragg, has appeared in a large body of films, including Disney's *The Lion King* (1994), *The Pink Panther 2* (2009), and the controversial *Lolita* (1997).

About the Actor:

Viggo Mortensen's family traveled a great deal and he spent several years living in Venezuela, Argentina, and Denmark.

"It's all in the reflexes."

Kurt Russell as Jack Burton – ***Big Trouble in Little China (1986)***

Setting:

After Burton throws his knife at David Lo Pan (James Hong) and misses, Lo Pan picks it up and throws it at Burton. He snatches the knife from the air and throws it back, killing Lo Pan, and causing thunder to clap and all the Buddha statutes to fall. This is his comment.

Movie Trivia:

The Coupe De Villes, that sing the song "Big Trouble in Little China" at the end of the movie, are a band consisting of John Carpenter, Nick Castle, and Tommy Lee Wallace.

About the Actor:

During the commentary on the DVD of *Big Trouble in Little China* (1986), Kurt Russell gets a big laugh watching himself go down the elevator after taking the "medicine" and saying, "I feel kind of invincible."

"I'll throw in about $1.60 worth of change if you can dig it out of old Bob there."

Kris Kristofferson as Billy the Kid – ***Pat Garrett and Billy the Kid (1973)***

Setting:

After Billy kills his captors, a man comes up with his horse. Billy tells him he is going to trade his horse for the buckskin horse the man is riding. Earlier, Bob Ollinger (R. G. Armstrong) threatened Billy with his shotgun that was loaded with 16 thin dimes. Billy used that shotgun to kill Bob, and offers the dimes as an addition to the horse he's trading for the buckskin.

Movie Trivia:

Kris Kristofferson fell in love with on-screen love interest Rita Coolidge, who played Maria, and the two were married shortly after filming.

About the Actor:

Kris Kristofferson married Rita Coolidge, his second wife, on August 17, 1973, two days after his divorce from Frances Beer, his first wife from February 1961.

"Oh, I wouldn't worry too much about that. We're professional police officers. We do this for a living."

Mel Gibson as Sergeant Martin Riggs – ***Lethal Weapon 2 (1989)***

Setting:

Riggs' reply to Arjen Rudd (Joss Ackland). When being arrested, Rudd tells Riggs, "You have no idea what you're doing."

Movie Trivia:

Lethal Weapon 2 (1989) was nominated for an Oscar in the Best Effects, Sound Effects Editing (Robert G. Henderson and Alan Robert Murray) category.

About the Actor:

Mel Gibson shares a birthday with J.R.R. Tolkien. Gibson was born on January 3, 1956. Tolkien on January 3, 1892.

"He ain't hard to recognize if you know what you're looking for."

Kevin Costner as Charley Waite – ***Open Range (2003)***

Setting:

Waite's reply to Boss Spearman (Robert Duvall), when Spearman asks if Waite would know the killer Butler (Kim Coates), if he saw him.

Movie Trivia:

In the movie *Open Range* (2003), Charley Waite (Kevin Costner) shares his full name, Charles Travis Postelwaite, and demands to know Boss Spearman's (Robert Duvall) real name in case they go to meet their maker. Spearman discloses his real name, Bluebonnett, and makes Waite swear to not tell anyone.

About the Actor:

Kevin Costner had a son, Liam, with girlfriend Bridget Rooney in 1996. Liam was the fourth of Costner's six children.

"You know brother, where I come from, the definition of death is emptiness. If that's the case, I've been dead for a long, long, long time."

Steven Seagal as Shane Daniels – ***A Dangerous Man (2009)***

Setting:

Daniels' reply during the final confrontation when the Colonel (Bryon Mann) says, "You want the old man? You pay with your life."

Movie Trivia:

Deboragh Gabler produced *A Dangerous Man* (2009). She is also the producer of *Dancing Ninja* (2010) starring Lucas Grabeel and David Hasselhoff.

About the Actor:

Steven Seagal is listed as one of seven Executive Producers for *A Dangerous Man* (2009). There were also four Associate Producers and one Co-executive Producer.

"What was that?"

Bruce Willis as John McClane – ***Die Hard With a Vengeance (1995)***

Setting:

McClane is searching among the containers of the ship Simon (Jeremy Irons) is using to attempt his getaway. He runs into a bad guy who says, "Necht schiessen!" It means "Don't shoot!" McClane puts two rounds into him and then asks the above to the body.

Movie Trivia:

A couple of the taglines for *Die Hard With a Vengeance* (1995) include: "Think fast. Look alive. Die Hard." "On a good day he's a great cop. On a bad day he's the best there is." "John McClane is about to have a very bad day."

About the Actor:

Bruce Willis enrolled in the drama program at Montclair State University.

To Be Continued...

INDEX

MOVIES

ACTORS

ABOUT THE AUTHOR

Alain Burrese is the author of *Hard-Won Wisdom From The School Of Hard Knocks*, eight instructional DVDs on martial arts and self-defense, a thriller titled *Lost Conscience*, and the *Tough Guy Wisdom* series. He is currently working on additional titles to the *Tough Guy Wisdom* series, another novel, additional instructional DVDs, and several other projects. Alain's background includes serving as a paratrooper with the 82nd Airborne Division, a sniper instructor for the 2nd Infantry Division, living and training in Japan and South Korea where he earned a 4th degree black belt in the self-defense art of Hapkido, teaching, bodyguarding, speaking, mediating, practicing law, security, and various other positions throughout the years. He currently lives in Montana with his wife and daughter, and when not with them, he spends his time writing, teaching, speaking, and helping others resolve conflict. That, and of course, watching tough guy movies.

TOUGH GUY WISDOM SERIES

Tough Guy Wisdom
Tough Guy Wisdom II: Return of the Tough Guy

Future Volumes:

Tough Guy Wisdom: John Wayne
Tough Guy Wisdom: Clint Eastwood
Tough Guy Wisdom: Charles Bronson
Tough Guy Wisdom: Chuck Norris
Tough Guy Wisdom: Sylvester Stallone
Tough Guy Wisdom: Arnold Schwarzenegger
Tough Guy Wisdom: Rise of the Super Heroes
Tough Guy Wisdom IV
Tough Guy Wisdom V
Tough Guy Wisdom VI …

www.ingramcontent.com/pod-product-compliance
Lightning Source LLC
LaVergne TN
LVHW010100110826
845155LV00028B/423